D0505226

Marye Cameron-Smith trained as a home economist at the Edinburgh College of Domestic Science before joining James A. Jobling, manufacturers of 'Pyrex' ovenglass, in Sunderland as assistant principal, then as principal of the Home Centre. In this centre the company organized training courses for store personnel selling 'Pyrex', and recipe work, testing new products, was carried out in the kitchen. She then moved to the London office and was involved in product public relations, and was concerned with the introduction of 'Pyrosil' in this country.

Her interest in frozen foods began when she joined Birds Eye Foods, first to set up a retail-store demonstration service, and then as manager of a new home-economics department. Because of this she was an early user of home freezers and recognized the advantage of these not only for freezing fresh or home-grown produce, but for the practicability of buying and storing large quantities of commercially frozen food.

Marye Cameron-Smith is now Cookery Editor of *Woman's Own*.

# Fresh from the Freezer

MARYE CAMERON-SMITH

PENGUIN BOOKS

Penguin Books Ltd, Harmondsworth, Middlesex, England
Penguin Books Inc., 7110 Ambassador Road, Baltimore,
Maryland 21207, U.S.A.
Penguin Books Australia Ltd, Ringwood, Victoria, Australia

First published 1969
Reprinted 1970 (three times)
Reprinted with revisions 1971
Copyright © Marye Cameron-Smith, 1969

Made and printed in Great Britain by
Cox & Wyman Ltd,
London, Reading and Fakenham
Set in Monotype Modern No. 1

# CONTENTS

# 1

# WHY FREEZE FOOD?

Hidden in the mists of time are stories of man's earliest efforts to preserve food from the harvest of plenty against the lean months when many die of starvation. Mankind alone, with the exception of a few animals like squirrels that store nuts, thinks of the future, and has sought ways of preserving food since the beginning of civilization as we know it today. Prehistoric man preserved his cereals by parching; his berries, nuts and fruit by drying. The American Indians dried their meat in the sun and made pemmican. The hunter learned to dry and salt his game and fish; samples of dried food found in Jericho have been estimated as being four thousand years old. During the thirteenth century the Venetian explorer, Marco Polo, is reported as finding the Tartars drying milk in goatskins suspended over their camp fires. For many centuries the techniques of food preservation were almost at a standstill or developed very slowly and were based on simple methods of fermentation, drying, smoking or curing with salt. In ancient times it was not appreciated that low- or high-temperature environments had any connexion with food storage. It was only when the biological causes of food spoilage became better known and understood that more advanced and more appropriate methods of preservation were developed.

Just as soon as fish are caught, animals slaughtered and vegetables and fruit harvested, life ends. The energy previously provided to maintain cell structure and growth and the ability to resist infection also comes to an end. One cause of food deterioration is activity by micro-organisms which are present everywhere in the form of yeasts, moulds and bacteria. Micro-organisms cause chemical changes by reproducing themselves at a rapid rate, absorbing essential materials and putting the waste products back into the food. The effects of these changes are associated with decay and putrefaction. Another reason for deterioration is the combination of certain chemical changes promoted by enzymes causing undesirable changes associated with 'off' flavours, deterioration in texture and loss of colour – particularly noticeable in stale vegetables, for example. The environment favouring the rapid development of these food-spoilage mechanisms is relatively high temperature and moisture. And even if these two main causes are controlled, chemical reactions in the food itself – for example oxidation in fatty foods – can lead to rancidity. The success and suitability of freezing as a simple method of food preservation is based on the destruction of the micro-organisms and the inactivation of the enzymes.

Other methods of preservation aim at the same objective by the use of high temperatures or by chemical means, but they usually cause some changes in either colour, flavour or texture, or more likely, a combination of these natural and desirable qualities.

Chemical preservation by salting, curing or pickling has only limited appeal because it makes fundamental changes to the original flavour and texture of the food. It nevertheless provides good, tasty food which is appreciated by most people in one form or another. Sterilization which uses high temperature followed by sealing in a can or bottle as a means of preservation also causes some changes to the original flavour, texture and colour. Napoleon, conscious of the importance of providing food for an army with long supply lines, used an idea put forward by Nicholas Appert in 1805, who preserved food by putting it into bottles which were sealed with corks and heated. Although some knowledge of food spoilage by bacteria was known at the time, it was left to an Englishman, Peter Durrand, to take out the first patent for preserving food in tin containers in 1810. However, the British did not accept this method too readily and the development of the canning industry centred in Boston, Massachusetts. It was not until the early 1920s that canned food (mainly fruit and vegetables) became more popular in this country. Of course, the main advantage of heat-treated bottled and canned foods is that they can be stored for long periods relatively cheaply.

Accelerated Freeze Drying – commonly known as A.F.D. – is a preservation technique combining both freezing and drying which requires complicated and costly engineering plant and is not a process that is likely to be used in the home. It is similar to the freeze-drying process used at the end of the Second World War for the production of pharmaceuticals and biological materials for medical use. The first penicillin and blood plasma were distributed in dried form after freeze-drying. More recently this process has been improved and applied to food, but is applicable only to a limited range of foods and is used commercially in the preparation of soups, vegetables, and some complete meals. A.F.D. foods, after processing, must be packed in airtight containers and are reconstituted with water when required for use. There are indeed quite a lot of fruits and vegetables which respond well to this method, in particular apples, and potatoes, often known as 'instant' potato. However, many partially and fully prepared foods and complete dishes can be successfully quick-frozen but are unsuitable for the more sophisticated drying process, if the natural flavour and texture are to be retained.

It follows that the use of refrigeration to freeze food as a method of storage provides the housewife with the best and most economical opportunity. Freezing at the correct low temperature results in foods which most closely resemble the original fresh foods in colour, flavour and texture. It is a method of preservation which can be understood and used without the need for complicated equipment in any home. It can be successfully applied to most raw and prepared cooked foods. Above all, a home freezer provides the means of making the fullest possible use of the increasing range and variety of commercially quick-frozen foods.

As a means of preserving food, refrigeration has become part of our everyday life and has been so for a long time. Nero, the Roman emperor, had slaves bring snow down from the mountain slopes. This was stored in cone-shaped pits lined with straw and leaves, and was kept to cool drinks and food during the summer. Alexander the Great lined trenches with snow and ice cut from rivers to cool kegs of wine which he gave to his soldiers on the eve of battle. Even in these early days it was recognized that snow and ice would make drinks more palatable in the summer and would, when used to pack around freshly killed meat or fish, delay deterioration for a short time.

By the middle of the nineteenth century ice became a much sought-after commodity, and clipper ships sailing from Boston in America carried cargoes of natural ice cut from ponds and lakes, packed in sawdust for sale in London, Lisbon, Bombay and Cairo. In fact, the refrigeration industry today owes a great debt to the merchant ship. The process we call mechanical refrigeration and which is now taken for granted in everyday life had its birth in 1834 with the invention of the vapour-compression machine by Jacob Perkins, an American engineer living in London. Carl von Linde, a German professor of thermodynamics, further developed the idea on a scientific basis and in 1895 published the various heat-engine cycles which could be used for the efficient mechanical production of cold. The German refrigeration company Linde produces food freezers today and supplies thousands of homes in Europe. The earliest applications of this new invention were on board cargo ships. Like so many great inventions, this one was born of necessity – that of providing the means of bringing food from overseas to feed the growing population of the British Isles. It was in the summer of 1880, after several years of costly trial and error, that the steamship *Strathleven* brought the first refrigerated cargo to the British Isles. Since then frozen lamb and mutton and chilled and frozen beef have been shipped from Australia, New Zealand and the Argentine to this country to meet a dietary necessity. Imported meat is popular because low temperature preserves the meat close to its original flavour and quality, long enough for it to be distributed in this country and overcomes the deterioration which would otherwise take place in the distance and time between source, market and consumer.

The temperature of melting snow and ice is 32°F (0°C) and if used to cool food will only delay the natural spoilage for relatively short periods. But once it was discovered that mechanical refrigeration could be designed to provide lower temperatures food could be kept fresh for much longer. Temperatures certainly no higher than 0°F ( − 18°C) are

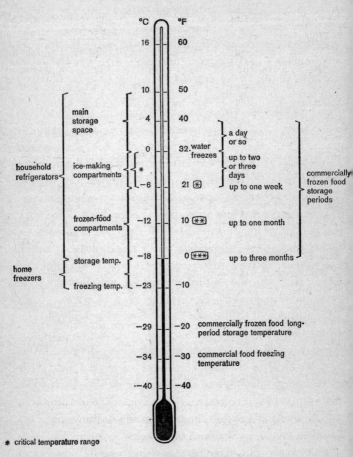

Frozen-food temperature chart

required for freezing in order to retain the true original flavour, colour and nutritional value of food if long periods of storage are required. It was only in 1924 that quick-freezing as we know it today was 'discovered'. Clarence Birdseye, an American scientist and explorer, when trapping for furs in Labrador, noted that the flavour and quality of fish caught from holes in the ice and frozen naturally in the very low Arctic temperatures was close to that of fish eaten the day it was caught, even after the fish had been in the low-temperature ice for months.

He concluded that the high quality of this fish was due to the fact that the fish was really fresh at the moment it was frozen and had been cooled very quickly to well below 0°F ($-18$°C), then held at low temperature during the Arctic winter.

The only difference between this natural way of preserving food and the process used today by quick-frozen food companies and home freezer owners is that extreme low temperatures are provided by mechanical refrigeration. By the early 1930s not only fish, but shell fish, poultry, vegetables, fruits and meat were being equally well preserved by the same commercial process in this country.

## QUICK-FREEZING

The effect of quick-freezing is to stop decay by slowing down the chemical and enzymatic reactions in the food so that it can be stored for reasonably long periods, and when quickly thawed, will be like the original food in colour, flavour and taste. Just how close to the quality of original fresh food, depends to a great extent upon how long the food being frozen is held in the critical temperature range between 32°F and 21°F (0°C and −6°C). The longer food is held in this temperature range during freezing, the more the eating-qualities of the food will be adversely affected. In this temperature range the equilibrium of water pressure within the cells of the food and in the intercellular spaces is particularly disturbed when food is being reduced in temperature – this is known to the food technologist as osmosis. If the temperature reduction is slow, water is lost from the cells and is added to ice forming between the cells, rather than forming ice crystals within the cells themselves. It is only when the reduction in temperature is so fast that there is little or no transference of water through the cell membrane walls that 'perfect' quick-freezing takes place and there is no physical damage to the cell wall.

Even in commercial quick-freezing this ultra-fast reduction in temperature is seldom achieved, but for practical and economic purposes commercial freezing gets close to it. Rapid thawing is desirable for similar reasons, and so recommendations are given for cooking vegetables, which are particularly prone to this effect, by plunging them into boiling water straight from the freezer. The amount of fluid, or 'drip', running from food on thawing is an indication of the change in the texture caused by slow freezing. The less the fluid lost the better the texture and the more enjoyable the eating quality will be.

In industry most food is frozen at temperatures not higher than −30°F (−34°C). More recently, some fruits are frozen at ultra low temperatures in liquid nitrogen or other suitable safe refrigerants, to ensure the best texture. It is for these reasons that an ice-making compartment and a frozen-food storage compartment in a household refrigerator will not give the best results if used for freezing food at home. They do not provide sufficiently low temperature to reduce the temperature of the food through the critical zone quickly enough. A food freezer which will provide a temperature of 0°F ( −18°C) or lower is specially designed for the purpose; while it will not, obviously, 'quick' freeze food, it will freeze fast enough to ensure a satisfactory eating quality.

Living in Britain, we do not have to be so concerned with food preservation in the home as in many other countries. Our climate is temperate – rarely very hot and rarely very cold. We have shops close to where we live. Our kitchens, particularly in modern houses and flats, tend to be small. We have a tradition of frequent shopping; most housewives still shop for food each day. These traditional habits generally mean that we have not needed to store food at home for very long. But as conditions change, new factors are influencing home food storage. We live in a society of increasing affluence, using more motor-cars, travelling more widely and more frequently, and using more and more labour-saving domestic appliances. Our small shops are slowly being replaced by larger food stores and supermarkets; our homes are better designed, many of them are centrally heated, and families have come to expect a wider choice of food from the housewife who is encouraged to buy an ever-increasing range of foods. The grocer today offers more than 6,000 different foods, compared with about 3,000 thirty years ago.

A freezer in the home to store home-produced and commercially packed frozen foods, means that food which is 'fresh because it is frozen' is available all the year round – fresh because it has been preserved at the peak of its quality by modern developments in food freezing.

# 2

## OWNING A HOME FREEZER

Even though there are about twice as many different kinds of foods in the average grocer's shop than there were thirty years ago, fundamental habits die hard and the kinds of food eaten at breakfast, lunch, tea and supper have changed very slowly. What has changed dramatically is the presentation of foods by the manufacturer and the grocer and their general availability all the year round. A study of production statistics shows that canned, packeted and frozen foods have altered buying patterns and changed the habits and attitudes of the consumer. In 1952 we were spending £540 million on 'convenience' foods, but by 1966 this had risen to £1,190 million, which in household terms means 4s. 7d. in every pound spent on food. This is an increase of 118 per cent; but particularly significant is that during this period the price of convenience foods rose by an average of only 27 per cent, compared with a rise of 71 per cent in food prices generally. These were the years in which the commercial frozen food business grew and developed. Between 1952 and 1966 expenditure on frozen foods rose by as much as 3,000 per cent, while prices on the whole did not rise significantly.

Our parents and grandparents can be forgiven for rejecting frozen foods when the quality of the food, the techniques of preparation, freezing and storage, and the type of equipment and method of handling in the retail shop were far below the minimum standards acceptable today. It is commonly believed that frozen foods are now equal in quality, or in some cases superior, to the best market-bought products. Frozen foods are a great deal more like fresh food than much of the food in shops which has been handled many times over and suffered in quality as a result.

Unfortunately the low-temperature chain of refrigeration which keeps good food fresh across oceans and continents to the point of sale has a weak link – the lack of suitable refrigeration equipment in the consumer's kitchen. The installation of a home freezer not only completes the chain, but makes for better-organized shopping and cooking.

## FREEZING SAVES TIME AND WORK

Owning a home freezer does not mean an end to retail food shopping, but it does mean that shopping expeditions can be planned to avoid the busiest and often the most expensive times in the shops on Fridays and Saturdays, and just before public holidays. Daily shopping for many foods can become weekly shopping, giving busy housewives more leisure time. Cooking and baking in larger quantities saves time and fuel. A favourite dish may require special ingredients that are perhaps not easy to obtain locally, or only in large quantities. Many dishes also take a long time to prepare. These can now be prepared in sufficient quantity for several meals – one can be served and the rest frozen and stored until needed. The time spent in preparation then becomes worth while.

The food freezer saves time and work when entertaining at home. If all the food has been prepared in advance, only last-minute preparations, cooking and serving are necessary. There are many dishes – appetizers, main dishes, vegetables, hot and cold sweets, and puddings – that can be partially or fully prepared and frozen, and then need only a short time to thaw or heat through. With a home freezer housewives at last become hostesses who relax and enjoy being with their guests, needing to spend only a little time in the kitchen.

As well as home-prepared foods there is now an ever-increasing variety of pre-frozen entrée dishes available in retail frozen-food cabinets though they are still somewhat expensive for everyday use. These have been prepared by experienced chefs working in commercial manufacturers' kitchens and only require heating through for a relatively short time. Supplemented with frozen vegetables, these dishes make the preparation of meals easy and speedy.

## FREEZING SAVES MONEY

Real economies can be made by freezing and storing seasonal foods. Farmers and families who live in agricultural areas and grow their own fruit and vegetables, shoot game and catch fish, have already discovered the financial savings of preserving these foods when in season and therefore at their highest quality. Most people are attracted by the economy of storing high-quality food available at low prices in time of abundance, particularly if the food is in season for only a few weeks or even days.

Food purchased in bulk from a market garden or small-holding is invariably cheaper than that purchased in smaller quantities from the local store. Large food purchases bring other advantages. They save time and energy later in the year by eliminating frequent shopping for small daily supplies of relatively expensive, perishable foods.

For the family with access to the 'bag' from hunting, shooting or fishing expeditions, freezers have special advantages – hare, grouse, duck, pheasant, salmon and trout need not be enjoyed for only a short period but, correctly prepared and frozen, can be brought out for special occasions some time after the season is over.

While the majority of commercial frozen-food manufacturers do not yet pack large cartons for retail sale, some of them do supply catering-pack sizes to selected retail stores and cash-and-carry distributors. These packs are usually in $2\frac{1}{2}$ lb., 5 lb. or 10 lb. sizes and contain vegetables, fruit or fish of the same high quality as in the smaller packs; but the price per pound is usually lower, making a saving of 10 per cent or more. If the larger packs are not available, some retailers will reduce the price of the smaller packs if several dozen or so of different kinds of food are purchased at one time. Some manufacturers introduce new foods at specially low prices and this is another time to replenish the freezer.

Inquiries from shops where home freezers are sold will often reveal the name of a local wholesaler or manufacturer, who will deliver commercially frozen food against a telephone order. If the order is substantial, say £5 or more, deliveries to your home may be made without additional charge. Harrods of Knightsbridge, London, for example, not only supply large catering-size packs of commercially frozen food, but will also supply cuts of freshly butchered meat in quantities as requested, packed, sealed and labelled ready for home freezing. Traditional English, French and most American cuts of meat are available, and local deliveries are made by van without charge and passenger train or air freight at additional cost. If there are any difficulties in finding a supplier of bulk packs of frozen foods, write to the Food Freezer Committee, 76 Jermyn Street, London SW1, who will supply the names and addresses of organizations who deliver bulk orders at wholesale prices.

Similar economies can be made by buying ice cream in half-gallon or gallon cans, or large cartons. There are many 'speciality' ice creams such as cassatas, melon surprise and sorbets, which are too large for just one meal and which are not usually available in single portions or family-block sizes. With a home freezer portions can be taken out and the rest held in store without wastage. Incidentally, the average American eats about 5 gallons of ice cream a year, while the average Briton eats only 1 gallon. But then 70 per cent of the ice cream sold in America is of the 'take home' variety which is kept in the freezer and used whenever required.

## FREEZING IS CONVENIENT

A well-stocked freezer, containing not only a variety of foods specially liked by the family but also some basic commodities such as bread, vegetables, fruit, fish and meat, will do away with fears that not enough food has been bought to carry through Easter, Christmas and Bank Holidays. There are no more problems when the family bring home friends, and no more excuses for stale bread and cold left-over joints in the larder. There can always be oven-fresh bread, cakes and tasty meat dishes in the freezer.

There must be many wives and mothers who, if they are to be away from home for a time, worry about what their families will eat. Here, too, food can be prepared before going away, labelled for each day, and there are few older children or husbands who could not quickly cook up a hot evening meal from prepared foods left in the freezer.

Preparing foods for picnics, long journeys or parties often means a very early rise if the food is to be prepared on the same day. With a freezer, sandwiches, snacks and meals can be prepared and frozen the day (or even days) before, and taken out in time to thaw before they are needed.

If there is a variety of food in the freezer, meal-planning becomes easier and meals more exciting, appetizing and nutritious. Because plans can be made in advance, a home freezer will save money and work, so that there is more time to enjoy hours of leisure.

Perhaps some of these advantages and suggestions will have already provoked many other ideas as to why there should be a freezer in every home.

# 3

# CHOOSING A HOME FREEZER

Relatively few families have a food freezer in their home; most of those are undoubtedly chest freezers, bought by families living in the country who are much more dependent upon adequate stocks of food at home than are city dwellers.

The sales of home freezers have been growing quickly, and about 250,000 are now sold each year. Their popularity was first slow to develop, partly because there was a limited choice of models, but principally because little is known about freezing as a means of preserving food. The intending purchaser has been restricted in the main to a few chest freezers which were basically ice-cream conservators, converted to home use by fitting a single lift-up counter-balanced lid. There has also been a limited range of upright freezers of about 15 to 20 cu. ft, imported from Canada and the U.S.A., which were relatively expensive.

The choice has now increased considerably, and contrary to popular belief many home freezers are neither large nor expensive. The range available varies in size from just under 2 to about 20 cu. ft. The most popular size is 5 to 6 cu. ft in capacity and priced about £75. With a wide range from which to choose, selecting the right freezer in type and size to suit the family purse and food requirements needs some thought. Because it is likely to be in the home for at least 7 years or more, it is wise to do a lot of looking and comparing before making a final decision.

Generally there are three quite different types of home freezers. They are:

(1) The upright freezer – or 'reach in'.

(2) The chest freezer or 'dive in'.

(3) The refrigerator/freezer – or 'combination'.

All these are available in a wide range of sizes, and each of the three types has its own advantages and disadvantages.

## UPRIGHT FREEZERS

Currently, there are many models from which to choose, varying in size from just below 2 to about 20 cu. ft. These are all fitted with a front-opening door and nearly all have fixed refrigerated shelves.

The advantage of this type of freezer is that it occupies the smallest floor area for each cubic foot of storage space and this may well be the deciding factor if the freezer is to be installed in a kitchen where floor space is at a premium. Several of the smaller models of about 2 cu. ft capacity are designed to stand on top of a household refrigerator or other appliance. The upright front-opening freezer gives quick access and easier stock control. Some models have additional narrow shelves fitted inside the door. These are useful for small packages of food which have been opened and partly used. If the main shelves are formed by refrigerant cooling coils, food will freeze faster because it is in immediate contact with the low-temperature surface. A few of the largest upright freezers are refrigerated by means of air circulated by a small fan and include automatic de-frosting. In these freezers the shelf height is usually adjustable and better use can therefore be made of the available space, especially if a lot of irregularly shaped packages such as poultry, joints of meat, etc., are to be frozen and stored.

The main, though not serious, disadvantage of the upright freezer is the loss of cold air every time the door is opened; it is not so much the small rise in air temperature that is important, but that the cold air is replaced by warm air containing moisture which is frozen out on the cooling coils. This means that the upright freezer, unless fitted with automatic de-frosting, may require more frequent de-frosting than the chest-type freezer. But, as the door of a home freezer is not opened very often, this disadvantage should not outweigh the obvious advantages of the upright freezer over other types. Some models are fitted with slide-out drawers on each refrigerated shelf; this arrangement does help to reduce the exchange of air when opening the door.

If there is any doubt about the strength of the floor on which the freezer is to stand, remember that an upright model will have greater floor loading than the equivalent capacity chest freezer. The approximate weight of the freezer when fully loaded can be obtained by adding the weight of the freezer itself to the weight of food it will hold, allowing 20 lb. of food for each cubic foot of storage space.

## CHEST FREEZERS

Many of the chest freezers, particularly those in the capacity range of 4 to 10 cu. ft, have been converted from commercial ice cream conservators and may well therefore be slightly cheaper than the equivalent upright freezer. Their particular advantage is that since they open from the top there is little loss of cold air when the lid is lifted, so they do not normally need to be de-frosted as frequently as upright freezers. For fast freezing, packaged foods must be placed against the side walls of the storage space, which may be inconvenient if the cabinet is already fairly heavily loaded. Most chest freezers are fitted with baskets which make it easier to handle the food – particularly food at the bottom of the chest – although they do of course reduce the effective storage space. Some chest freezers have a separate small compartment for the actual freezing, after which the frozen food can be transferred to the main storage compartment. Others are fitted with a fast-freezing switch and warning light, which in the 'on' position allows the refrigeration unit to run continuously by shorting out the thermostat. This switch should be returned to the normal position after each batch of food has been frozen at a lower temperature.

A chest freezer occupies a greater floor space for each cubic foot of capacity than an upright, though this may not be important if it is installed in an outhouse, garage or cellar.

Few, if any, chest-type freezers are fitted with automatic de-frosting, and even though de-frosting is only necessary two or three times a year with normal use – it is a much more strenuous and tiresome job on a chest freezer than an upright. Some of the large chest freezers – even when fitted with baskets – are very deep. This makes stock rotation and access to particular packages much more difficult. The storage space tends to become an untidy jumble, causing damage to packaging and frustration to the housewife! It is exactly for these reasons that many of the large food stores and supermarkets are installing multi-deck frozen-food sales cases – to replace the older bin-type cabinets. These vertical cases provide easy access for the shopper to the packet of her choice and enable the grocer to check his stock at a glance. Similar arguments apply equally well to the home freezer – most housewives prefer to stock their canned and packeted foods on a shelf in the pantry rather than on top of each other in a timber chest!

## REFRIGERATOR/FREEZER

These should not be confused with domestic refrigerators which have relatively small ice-boxes or frozen-food storage compartments. The refrigerator/freezer is generally designed with separate external doors to each section. The freezer may be located above or below the main refrigerator in models up to about 15 cu. ft capacity or in larger models may have a separate full-length door alongside the refrigerator door.

The advantage of the refrigerator/freezer is that chilled and frozen foods are stored in one place. They are normally located in the kitchen or pantry as the refrigerator section is used fairly frequently. If there is only one refrigeration unit for the combination, on a cubic-foot basis, they may be cheaper to run than the other types. Refrigerator/freezers are available in combined capacities from 6 to 40 cu. ft and the freezer capacity is normally not less than one quarter of the total storage capacity. The freezer space is much greater than this – up to one half of the total – in some of the larger models manufactured in Canada, the U.S.A. and Sweden, where refrigerator/freezers are the most popular.

Having first decided on the type of food freezer likely to be most suitable, next choose the best size; although this may well be determined by the cost, many other factors need to be considered to suit individual needs and circumstances.

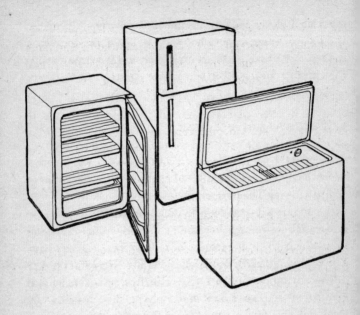

## CAPACITY

Each cubic foot of usable space will store about 20 lb. of food. In the U.S.A., where 68 lb. per head of frozen foods are bought per year, compared with 12 lb. in Britain, the recommendation on size is 6 cu. ft per person. On this basis the appropriate capacity of food freezer for the average British family will be over 2 cu. ft per person. This is likely to be increased for families living in the country, who shop less frequently and possibly have readier access to home-grown food. It may well be less for families living in towns and for those with smaller kitchens and a good selection of food shops nearby. The average size per person should be doubled for those who do a lot of entertaining, or who enjoy time-consuming hobbies and activities outside the home, and those who for any reason benefit from preparing meals several weeks ahead. Whatever size is finally selected, it is better to 'size up' rather than 'size down'. Once there is a food freezer in the home, more and more use will be made of it, and more uses found for it. A home freezer should have a useful life of at least ten years. Generally the higher the capacity, the lower is the cost per cubic foot.

## THE COST OF BUYING FREEZER SPACE

Upright freezers cost about £24 per cu. ft for small capacity freezers of about 2 cu. ft. The cost drops to about £15 per cu. ft for capacities in the range 5–6 cu. ft and reduces still further to about £12 per cu. ft for capacities of 15 cu. ft and larger. Chest-type freezers are somewhat lower in initial cost, starting about £14 per cu. ft for capacities of about 4 cu. ft.

It is much more difficult to give guidance on the likely cost of a refrigerator/freezer, but the few British-made two-door combinations of relatively small capacity (total capacity about 12 cu. ft) cost about £11 per cu. ft of total space provided. Most of the larger combinations up to about 25 cu. ft vary between £16 and £20 per cu. ft, and the majority of these are imported from the U.S.A. or Canada and incorporate automatic de-frosting and other features such as automatic ice-cube makers and in the main storage compartments 'slide-out' drawers for meat, vegetables etc. On this basis it is still cheaper to buy a separate household refrigerator and freezer, choosing the size and type best suited to individual household needs.

All refrigerators and freezers designed and sold specifically for household use are subject to Purchase Tax, and the prices given above may well rise or fall according to the level of tax. Some retailers have freezers of the upright and chest type available for commercial use. They are normally of at least 14 cu. ft capacity and do not carry Purchase Tax; but it is necessary to satisfy the retailer that the purchase is being made for commercial use – e.g., a boarding house, nursing home, or for a farm, where food must be provided for staff and employees.

PERFORMANCE

There is as yet no British Standard Specification against which the ability of a home freezer to freeze a specified quantity of food in a certain time can be measured. There will no doubt be a Standard in due course, but in the mean-time one must rely on the performance claimed by the manufacturer. Before buying any particular model it is important to establish that it was in fact designed not just to *store*, but to *freeze* food. If necessary this can be done by ascertaining what quantity of food measured by weight and size can be reduced in temperature down to 0°F ( −18°C) in a specified time. The important temperature range is 32°F to 21°F (0°C to −6°C) (see Chapter 1, page 14) and the freezer should be capable of reducing the temperature of the specified amount of food through this temperature range in less than 12 hours and down to 0°F ( −18°C) in less than 24 hours. When freezing food the temperature in the freezer ideally should not rise above 0°F (−18°C), otherwise there will be some loss in quality and a reduction in the high-quality storage life of any food already frozen.

There is a British Standard Specification which covers the electrical safety and minimum general constructional requirements of household refrigerators. This is British Standard Specification No. 3456, part 11, and it is recommended that the freezer selected should be marked as complying with this standard.

## RUNNING COSTS

The cost of running a home freezer, excluding maintenance costs, depends upon a number of factors, any of which could make quite a difference to the approximation given. The factors influencing the running costs are: the local electricity charge, the size of the refrigerating unit which is related to the size of the freezer, the frequency of door or lid opening, the weight of food which is to be frozen each day, the temperature of the air surrounding the freezer and the effectiveness of the insulation. It is only possible to give a guide to the likely cost, but most manufacturers will give a rough estimate of the power likely to be consumed by their appliance per day. The popular size of home freezer, about 4 cu. ft, will consume about 1½ to 2 units per day and would therefore cost between 9p and 10p per week, assuming an electricity charge of 0·8p per unit. A freezer of half this capacity will normally consume more than half this power and a freezer of double the capacity will cost rather less than double the example quoted.

While the running cost is about double that of an equiva-

lent size of refrigerator, it works out on average at less than
½p per day for each 20 lb. of high-quality foods in the freezer –
certainly not an expensive outlay for the enjoyment and
benefits such a variety of food provides.


## INSTALLATION OF THE FREEZER

The important consideration when deciding where to put the
freezer is that it should be absolutely level, so that the cabinet
is not distorted. This will ensure that the lid (in the case of a
chest freezer) or the front opening doors (in an upright or
combination freezer) will close evenly on the door seal. The
site should be well ventilated, especially round the refriger-
ation-unit compartment, which is normally at the back, and
the running cost will be lower if it is sited in a cool, but not
damp, place. A 13 or 15 amp. power point will be required
adjacent to the freezer position. If this is not already there
it is advisable to check with the local Electricity Board
before arranging for additional power points to be put in.


## CARE OF THE FREEZER

Most freezers carry a five-year guarantee for the refrigeration
unit and the cabinet itself is guaranteed for one year. These
details will be given on the guarantee card supplied with each
new freezer. Most manufacturers supply a user's booklet,
and instructions for care and maintenance should be followed.
Generally advice and recommendations on how to de-frost
and what to do in case of power failure will be given, but the
following is a guide in their absence.

## DE-FROSTING

Frost will eventually form near the lid or door seal and on the walls and shelves of the freezer. Frost or ice which forms on the lid or door should be removed as soon as it appears because it will prevent the lid or door sealing correctly and will result in air leakage, allowing more frost to accumulate inside the freezer. The refrigeration unit will run for longer periods than necessary and increase the running costs. Continuous frost or ice formation on the door seal probably means that the gasket is not sealing correctly. This could be because the freezer is not standing on a level surface, that the gasket has been damaged or incorrectly fitted, or that the lid or door has been twisted.

General de-frosting of the whole of the inside of the freezer should be done when the frost is between $\frac{1}{4}$ in. and $\frac{1}{2}$ in. thick. This normally occurs about two or three times a year, but it does very much depend on how frequently the freezer door is opened and how long it is left open on each occasion.

To de-frost, food should be removed and packed as compactly as possible and, ideally, temporarily stored in a household refrigerator. Otherwise, it should be wrapped in several layers of newspaper or in aluminium foil and put in the coolest place available. After switching off the power supply a good deal of the frost can be removed by brushing or scraping – but only with a plastic or wooden tool; never under any circumstances should a sharp metal tool or a wire brush be used. A bowl of warm water placed in the freezer helps in the de-frosting process. The inside should be wiped with a solution of warm water with bicarbonate of soda (one tablespoon of bicarbonate of soda to each quart of water) followed by a final wipe with a clean cloth. After thorough

...he freezer should be switched on and allowed to run ...il the temperature is below 30°F ( −1°C) before being repacked with frozen food. This is probably a good time to clean the outside surfaces; a good quality refrigerator polish should be used according to the manufacturer's instructions.

## 'FROST-FREE' FREEZERS

Some of the larger and more expensive freezers are equipped with automatic de-frosting devices. These do not of course need manual de-frosting, but it is advisable to give them a thorough cleaning every six months or so. After disconnecting the freezer from the power supply, all food should be re-moved and held temporarily in a cool place, as suggested above. The interior can then be wiped down with a mild bicarbonate of soda solution (unless the manufacturer advises otherwise). Again allow the freezer to cool down to at least 30°F ( −1°C) or so before replacing the food.

## RE-LOADING THE FREEZER

An excellent time to check the food in store is while waiting for the freezer to cool before re-loading. Note any packaging which may be faulty and put food which has been longest in storage at the top of the chest or at the front of the shelves, to ensure that this will be used first.

It is also as well to remember that no matter how much care is taken of the frozen stock, there will normally be a small temperature rise, and if this is prolonged it will make a marginal reduction to the high-quality storage life. If the freezer is de-frosted infrequently – say once or twice a year – the effect of a small temperature fluctuation will not be detected in loss of flavour, colour, or taste; but it will be more marked on those foods which have a relatively short storage life, such as ice cream, oily fish and cooked meats. These foods should be protected from any temperature rise as much as possible.

# 4

# FROZEN-FOOD STORAGE IN HOUSEHOLD REFRIGERATORS

By the end of 1970 about 66 per cent of British homes had a refrigerator in the kitchen, but, as might be expected, ownership is higher in the south than in the north of England and in Scotland. One estimate shows that it varies from about 72 per cent of homes in the London area to as little as 38 per cent in Scotland. The households buying frozen foods follow a similar geographical pattern, from over 75 per cent in the London area to under 60 per cent in Scotland. It is possible to store proprietary frozen foods in the ice-making or frozen-food compartment of all household refrigerators, but the storage time depends upon the temperature that can be maintained in the compartment – the lower the temperature, the longer the recommended storage time. These compartments, usually located at the top of most refrigerators, are not normally designed for freezing food and should therefore not be compared with a genuine home freezer or with the freezer section of a 'combination' model.

To guide refrigerator owners on the storage times for frozen foods in these compartments a star-marking scheme was introduced in 1964 and published as British Standard No. 3739. Nearly all British-manufactured and some imported refrigerators comply with this standard and have either one, two or three stars in a curved frame on the door of the frozen-food compartment. Nearly all Birds Eye, for example, and some other frozen-food companies' packs are

marked with similar stars and show the high-quality storage
life in star-marked compartments. The storage period on the
packet makes allowances for any slight softening which might
have occurred during the carry-home time.

| In a compartment marked: | the temperature is not higher than: | and the average storage life for proprietary frozen foods is: |
| --- | --- | --- |
| ✳ | 21°F (−6°C) | up to 1 week |
| ✳ ✳ | 10°F (−12°C) | up to 1 month |
| ✳ ✳ ✳ | 0°F (−18°C) | up to 3 months |

The compartment temperatures given assume an average kitchen temperature and
a thermostat setting recommended by the refrigerator manufacturer.

The storage life of frozen foods varies from one kind of food
to another and some foods, for example cream cakes, oily fish
and various prepared cooked foods, have a shorter high-
quality storage life than given in the above table because of
their high fat content. Ice cream, and in particular dairy ice
cream, is especially heat sensitive and any substantial rise
in temperature above 10°F (−12°C) will soon result in softening, shrinkage and loss of texture. The approximate storage
time for proprietary ice cream in a compartment marked with
three stars is up to one month, with two stars up to one week
and one star about one day.

Although star marking is exclusively a method of indicating the storage time for commercially frozen foods and ice cream, it is possible to home-freeze small quantities of food in some compartments which will maintain 0°F ( −18°C) – but *only* if the refrigerator manufacturer gives specific instructions to do so. If a three-star compartment is not designed to freeze food, any warm food placed in this section will raise the temperature and adversely affect any other frozen food already in store.

For older refrigerators manufactured before 1964, and others without star-marked compartments, it is very difficult to give precise recommendations for the storage time of frozen foods. All that can be said is that firstly proprietary frozen foods should keep for up to three days in the ice-making compartment providing the temperature is higher than 21°F ( −6°C); and secondly, if the users' instruction book indicates the temperature which can be held in the ice-making compartment at a particular thermostat setting, an indication of the storage period can be obtained by referring to the temperature/time life given earlier in this chapter.

## DE-FROSTING FROZEN-FOOD STORAGE COMPARTMENTS

To remove frost and ice from the sides and base of a storage compartment the temperature of the metal must obviously be raised above 32°F (0°C) and thus the temperature of any frozen-food packs will also rise. Such a rise in temperature will not substantially affect the storage life of the food unless it is prolonged or is repeated frequently during the storage period. It is always advisable if possible to limit the temperature rise of any frozen-food packs whenever de-frosting is carried out. The best time to de-frost is when only a small quantity of food is being stored, or when any ice cream in the compartment is to be used within an hour or so of removal for de-frosting.

*Refrigerators which must be manually de-frosted*

The power should be switched off and the plug removed from the socket before de-frosting the ice-making or frozen-food storage compartment with the main refrigerator door open. Any frozen food in the compartment should be removed, wrapped in several layers of newspaper and kept in a cool place. The de-frosting time can be shortened by placing trays of warm water in the empty compartment and by using a wooden spatula to ease off the ice. The whole of the inside of the refrigerator should be thoroughly dried before the power is reconnected and switched on. If the refrigerator is fitted with a plate designed to collect the frost and ice below the ice-making compartments, only this plate need be removed and de-frosted. In this case it is of course not necessary to remove frozen food from the storage compartment. The frequency of de-frosting will depend upon how the refrigerator is used, but, on average, it should not be necessary more than once every two or three weeks or even longer. As most refrigerators which require manual de-frosting are fitted with one- or two-star frozen-food compartments, de-frosting once or twice every two or three weeks will not significantly affect the storage life of frozen foods providing that they are not allowed to thaw during the de-frosting period.

*Refrigerators with semi-automatic de-frosting*

The ice-making or frozen-food compartments in refrigerators with semi-automatic de-frosting are normally fitted with a push button which has to be pressed to start the de-frosting period. The refrigerating unit switches on again automatically after the frost and ice has melted and drained from the compartment. Depending upon the method of supplying heat to the compartment, it may take as little as half an hour or as much as several hours to de-frost. In the latter case the storage life of any frozen food which rises in temperature for several hours may be reduced, but if push-button de-frosting is carried out when there is only a small amount of food in the compartment and only once every few weeks, the food will not be adversely affected. In most cases it is advisable to wrap packets of frozen food in several thicknesses of newspaper and keep them in a cool place while the refrigerator is de-frosted. Again the compartment and interior of the refrigerator should be thoroughly dried before the unit returns to normal operation.

In some refrigerators, the main storage space is cooled by a plate located on the rear or side wall and when the push button is pressed only this part is de-frosted, the frozen-food compartment remaining unaffected. If this is so, then frozen food may of course be left in the compartment while the main storage space de-frosts. However, the frozen-food compartment should be manually de-frosted once every two or three months depending upon usage, and when this is done the recommendations for manual de-frosting given above should be followed.

*Refrigerators with fully automatic de-frosting*

Some of the larger refrigerators, especially those imported
from the U.S.A., are cooled by means of a fan circulating
cold air to the frozen-food compartment and to the main
storage space. In most of these refrigerators any frost or
ice collects on the cooling coil, which is located away from
the frozen-food compartment and main storage space. This
cooling coil is de-frosted automatically, usually several
times a day, by warm refrigerant gas or electrical heat,
without significantly affecting the temperature in the frozen-
food compartment and main storage space – so de-frosting has
no adverse effect on the storage life of the food.

However, if the frozen-food storage compartment is
raised in temperature several times a day in other types of
refrigerators fitted with fully automatic de-frosting devices
which warm up the compartment itself, any frozen food in
store is likely to fluctuate in temperature and its storage life
will be reduced.

## THAWED COMMERCIALLY FROZEN FOOD

Any frozen food which has thawed – its temperature will be
about $25°F$ ( $-4°C$) or higher – should be treated as perishable
and used within a reasonably short period of time. It should
not be re-frozen. There is no 'danger' in re-freezing food
which has been thawed for a short time, but slow freezing
in a frozen-food storage compartment will reduce much of the
original flavour, colour and texture, and it may well be
unpalatable for this reason.

# 5

# BUYING FROZEN FOODS

Although the commercial quick-freezing of food was in use in this country in the thirties, it was not until the immediate post-war years that quick-frozen foods became established. Today more and more housewives are buying frozen foods, realizing that apart from their convenience and value for money they are fresh and nutritious. The consumption of quick-frozen food in the U.S.A. averages about 68 lb. per head of population, in Sweden about 23 lb. and in the U.K. just under 12 lb. at the time of writing. In comparing U.K. consumption with that in the U.S.A. and Sweden, the facilities to store frozen foods at home must be taken into account. In this country most frozen foods are still bought for almost immediate consumption – though the pattern is changing, and by the late 1970s the purchase of quick-frozen food may well be double what it is today; by then the facilities to store at home in household refrigerators and home freezers will have improved.

The increasing popularity of frozen foods is due to their high quality, and this depends not only upon the speed of freezing but also upon the selection of only the freshest raw materials. Most of the frozen-food producers' factories are located in agricultural areas and at fishing ports, where the best vegetables and fish are available. After quick freezing, frozen food is stored in large refrigerated cold-stores and held at temperatures well below 0°F (−18°C) until required for distribution to regional depots and then to the retail shop. Great care is taken during distribution that the food temperature never rises much above 0°F ( −18°C), and insulated vehicles cooled by mechanical refrigeration plant or by solid carbon dioxide (dry ice) are used to move the food from cold-store to shop cabinet.

There are still a great many frozen-food cabinets in retail shops which are too small in display area and capacity to show a full range of frozen foods and ice cream, and others which, regrettably, do not provide sufficiently low temperatures for packaged frozen food and ice cream to be displayed in the top part of the cabinet. There is a new British Standard Specification No. 3053, which states that frozen foods at the load line should be held at a temperature not above +5°F ( −15°C), but not all retail cabinets comply with this minimum performance standard. Those that do are marked with a load limit line at each end of the frozen-food cabinet and with the number of this standard.

If frozen food is being purchased in quantity from a retail shop for storage in a home freezer, it is advisable to choose packages from well below the marked load lines, where the air temperature is lower. Select packages which are clean and firm and make sure that the packing is not torn or crushed. Frozen food that has been exposed as a result of damaged wrapping will dry out and lose flavour during storage. Buy frozen foods last when shopping, to shorten the time they will be without refrigeration. The retailer will normally wrap them (several layers of newspaper or equivalent insulating material) to reduce the temperature rise on the way home. If reasonable care is taken and the journey home is not unduly long, they will not have thawed before arrival. Do

not carry frozen foods in the boot of a car on a warm day!
Even if the carrying home time is about an hour and the
day is warm, most packages of frozen food will not suffer too
much – a little softening will not reduce the optimum storage
period marked on the packet, provided the food has not actu-
ally thawed. The more frozen food is purchased at one time
and packed tightly together on the journey home, the less
will be the temperature rise. Ice cream, sorbets, mousse and
similar foods will soften more quickly than other foods. They
should be packed between other foods, so that they are better
protected until they are stored in the freezer.

Some of the larger department stores sell pliable rec-
tangular-shaped insulated bags with carrying handles.
Insulex Ltd, 124 Barlby Road, London W10, manufacture
insulated bags in two sizes, 12 × 8 × 6 ins. and 14 × 10 × 6 ins.,
both fitted with a zip-closing lid. This type of insulated bag
gives good protection to frozen foods, particularly to ice
cream, and is strongly recommended if the journey home is
likely to be long. When arriving home, it is a good idea to
lower the temperature of the food as quickly as possible by
placing the packages in contact with a refrigerated surface
in the freezer or in the star-marked frozen-food storage compartment of a household refrigerator.

Although there will always be those who use only so-called
'fresh' market vegetables and other foods, most people are
buying increasing quantities of commercially frozen foods.
While nothing will quite equal fresh vegetables straight from
the farm or garden, many vegetables found in our shops
today have travelled so long through wholesale markets that
there is very little 'freshness' left by the time they are cooked.

There is an ever-increasing variety of commercially frozen

foods displayed and stored in retailers' cabinets under several well-known brand names, and there will always be particular brands and packs which are preferred to others. The space in the retailer's frozen-food cabinet is so valuable to him and to the frozen-food wholesalers and producers that there is little chance for packs which are not generally liked and which do not have a ready sale. It may help, however, to ask the retailer for a full list of foods which he could obtain from frozen-food companies. There is an extensive range of commercially frozen packs of vegetables, fruit, fish, meat, poultry, dairy and confectionery goods and prepared dishes and they are often available in two or three different sizes.

There are continuous deletions and additions as manufacturers improve older recipes and introduce new lines, including speciality foods such as crêpes suzette, lobster newburg, goulash, coq au vin and bouillabaisse, which can be found in the larger grocers shops, supermarkets and department stores. Be on the look-out too for different types of fish, meat and confectionery which are becoming more freely available in large catering packs through some wholesalers, cash-and-carry warehouses, and frozen-food distribution depots.

COOKING BOUGHT FROZEN FOODS

Most frozen food can be taken from the packet and cooked while still frozen. There may indeed be a loss of flavour and texture if juices run out of the food during a long thawing period. But there are exceptions to this – the important ones being dense, close-textured foods like poultry and game.

Large chickens, turkeys and ducks should be thoroughly thawed before cooking; this will take 24–48 hours depending on the weight of the bird. If they are not thawed properly the outside will be cooked and the inside flesh still raw. Individual pieces of poultry such as quarters and joints can be cooked while still hard, as they are usually grilled or fried with medium heat so that they do cook right through. If they are to be coated with egg and breadcrumbs it is advisable to thaw them slightly so that the coating will adhere. Pieces of poultry are particularly useful in casseroles and curries and, again, need not be thawed provided the cooking time is relatively long.

*Fish*

Some frozen-food producers now pack fish fillets in interleaving polythene film so that the fillets can be separated while still frozen and the individual fillets cooked straight from the pack. If fillets are not wrapped in this way the block-frozen pack must be partially thawed so that the fillets can be separated without breaking. Fish is also packed in 'steak' and pre-formed 'steak' form. Salmon and halibut steaks in individual portions need no thawing, nor do the pre-formed 'steaks' which are either moulded or cut from block-frozen fillets.

An increasing variety of food, particularly fish and meat in gravy, is packed in 'boil-in-bag' form. Kippers and smoked haddock, often containing a portion of butter, are packed in polythene bags which can be placed straight into a saucepan of boiling water and cooked for about 10 minutes.

*Meat*

There is a wide range of meat products most of which are excellent in quality and good value for money, particularly as all the trimming, mincing, mixing with onion and seasoning and the preparation of sauces and gravies has been completed. Such products as beefburgers, steakburgers, meat balls, faggots, sliced meat in gravy and roast meat dinners complete with vegetables can be cooked or heated up very quickly without thawing.

*Vegetables*

Frozen vegetables should be cooked for a short time in the minimum quantity of water. 'Free-flow' vegetables can be poured from the carton or bag, using only the quantity required. If block-frozen, the whole block should be placed in the recommended amount of boiling, salted water and cooked for not longer than the specified time (timing from when the water comes back to the boil). Because vegetables have been blanched before freezing, the cooking time is shorter than for market produce. Frozen vegetables can be steamed or cooked in the oven instead of boiled. For steaming, place the block in a steamer over a saucepan of boiling water which has, perhaps, other vegetables cooking in it. For oven cooking, place the block of vegetables on a piece of foil, add a little butter, salt and pepper, wrap over the foil to make a loose parcel and place on a baking tray. They will take slightly longer to cook – about 30 minutes for peas and 40 minutes for other vegetables. This method is ideal if the oven is already in use for a roast or casserole.

Potato chips, croquettes, etc., can be cooked or heated

without first being thawed by frying them in hot fat or baking them in the oven according to the manufacturer's instructions.

## Pastry and pies

Shortcrust and puff pastry should be thawed before use, so that it can be rolled out. Keep the pastry in the packet or wrapping while thawing, which will only take about an hour in an average kitchen temperature.

Sausage rolls and ready prepared fruit, meat and poultry pies in foil dishes do not require thawing and can go straight into a hot oven for the recommended baking time.

## Confectionery, fruit and ice cream

Cakes, e.g. cream sponges, gateaux and éclairs, are already baked, but should be allowed to thaw for an hour or so before being eaten. It is easier to cut cream-filled cakes while they are still hard; this way they will also take a shorter time to thaw. Fruit which is to be served cold, such as strawberries and raspberries, needs to be thawed, but takes only about an hour. Strawberries quickly lose their shape and texture after thawing and should not be taken out of the freezer too long before serving. If the fruit has been packed without sugar, sprinkle a little over the fruit while it is thawing so that it will form a syrup.

Take ice cream out of the freezer about 10 minutes before serving, so that it is slightly softened. While ice cream should be stored at 0°F ( −18°C) or lower, the ideal serving temperature is a little higher to bring out the best texture and flavour.

There should be few difficulties over the cooking of commercially frozen foods as most companies give adequate instructions – cooking directions, times and oven temperatures, and sometimes, serving suggestions – on the packet. The larger and well-known frozen-food companies employ experienced home economists who spend considerable time working out the best way to cook each product. The recommendations on the packet can therefore be relied on and should be followed, especially if the product hasn't been tried before.

# 6

# HIGH-QUALITY STORAGE LIFE OF FROZEN FOODS

Of all the questions asked about home freezing the one about the length of storage time of any particular type of food is the most frequent and is probably the most difficult to answer precisely. The storage life of food should be correctly described as the high-quality storage life. This, for all practical purposes, is the length of time until perceptible changes occur in colour, flavour or texture between food immediately *after* freezing and similar food which has been frozen and stored at low temperature. As far as home freezing is concerned the storage temperature should be 0°F ( −18°C) or lower and all recommendations for high-quality storage life assume storage at this temperature. It is important that only foods in excellent condition at the time of freezing have been chosen. Beef should not have been hung for too long, otherwise the fat may go rancid during storage. Use only really fresh fish and shellfish, fresh fruit and vegetables, for the longest high-quality storage time. Similarly pre-cooked foods should be removed from the heat before they reach the 'well-done' stage in order to obtain the longest high-quality storage period.

The high-quality storage life depends upon many factors as well as quality and temperature and it varies considerably between different types of food stored at the same temperature. Peas have a high-quality storage life up to 12 months at 0°F (—18°C-) and bacon less than two weeks at the same temperature. Certain other foods may store without detectable changes for 1 year at 0°F ( −18°C), five months at 5°F ( −15°C) but only one month at 15°F ( −9°C). Thus any rise in temperature above 0°F in a home freezer will shorten the optimum high-quality storage life by an amount related to the time it is above 0°F. This is known as the time–temperature–tolerance (T.T.T.) as it relates to frozen-food quality. Widely fluctuating temperatures during storage cause ice crystals to grow, and this too will normally reduce the high-quality storage period particularly of ice creams, sorbets and sauces. The effectiveness of packaging is important too. Inadequate packaging will not protect food from desiccation and oxidation during storage.

It may well be asked why the indications given for the high-quality storage life for home-frozen food are longer than the storage periods given on packets of commercially frozen food when held in a 3-star frozen-food compartment of a household refrigerator.

Commercial processors of quick-frozen foods are able to control the growing conditions and harvesting of fruit and vegetables and the buying of fish at the quayside and can therefore obtain really fresh produce. They are constantly improving methods of handling, processing, quick-freezing and packaging, and the *absolute* high-quality storage life at the time the food enters the factory cold-store, in which the temperature is below −20°F ( −29°C), is undoubtedly longer than the storage period for similar foods frozen at home. However, commercially quick-frozen foods are invariably subjected to further handling and exposed to consequent temperature fluctuations during distribution and in the retailers' frozen-food cabinets. In making an assessment of the balance of high-quality storage life of products in the retailers' cabinets the manufacturers take into account the cumulative loss and allow for a further temperature rise during the carrying-home time. The time given on their packets for storage in the frozen-food compartment of a household refrigerator may well therefore be shorter than for home-frozen foods. So far as home freezers are concerned, provided the temperature is maintained at 0°F ( −18°C) or below, the high-quality storage life of commercial quick-frozen food will be the same as that shown on the packet for a 3-star frozen-food compartment of a household refrigerator.

# HOW MUCH AND WHEN TO FREEZE

There is, of course, a limit to the amount of food which can be frozen at any one time. The limiting factor is the ability of the refrigeration unit to draw heat from the packaged unfrozen food and at the same time to maintain a temperature of not higher than 0°F (−18°C). It is for this reason that most household refrigerators and some ice cream conservators are not recommended for home freezing. These are normally designed to deal only with heat losses through the insulation and they don't have sufficient power to extract heat from unfrozen food and to maintain 0°F (−18°C) in the storage space.

Although food freezers are specifically designed to deal with these heat losses it is still not advisable to overload the freezer with food to be frozen. As explained in Chapter 3, the critical temperature zone when freezing food is between 32°F (0°C) and 21°F (−6°C), when the majority of the latent heat is being withdrawn. It is important to cool the food through this zone as quickly as possible, and this can only be done if the refrigeration system is powerful enough.

Most manufacturers give advice as to the quantity of new food which should be frozen at one time; this normally works out at 10 per cent of the freezer capacity or 2 lb. of food per day for each cubic foot of usable freezer space.

There are a number of things which can be done to ensure that food is frozen as rapidly as the freezer will permit. In chest-type freezers new packages should be placed against one of the side walls so that they are in close contact with the lowest temperature surface. There should be some space around the remaining sides of each new package to allow the low temperature air to circulate. In upright freezers fitted with refrigerated shelves, the same principle applies, except that the unfrozen pack should stand directly on the refrigerated shelf, preferably placing the flattest and largest surface area against the shelf. In larger freezers fitted with air-circulating fans, a free circulation of air should be allowed all round each pack to be frozen.

The rate of freezing depends upon the quantity of food put in the freezer at one time – the smaller the quantity the faster the rate of freezing. It also depends upon the thickness of the package. The thinner the package, the faster it will be frozen. For example, a thin carton of fruit or vegetables will freeze in a shorter time than a joint of meat or a chicken. While food is being frozen the door of the freezer should be opened as little as possible, to avoid raising the temperature. Twenty-four hours is advised by most manufacturers as the time required to freeze food down to the storage temperature. After freezing, the hard packages can be stacked tightly together in another part of the freezer to leave room for the next batch of food.

Most freezers are fitted with a cold-control or thermostat which regulates the temperature of air when turned to different settings. These settings may be letters, numbers or words describing the position, for example, 'storage' and 'freezing' or 'minimum', 'normal' and 'maximum'. When freezing food, have the control knob turned to the lowest temperature setting; for storage it can then be returned to the normal position.

*Table 1  Seasons of home-grown and some imported vegetables and fruit*

|  | VEGETABLES | FRUITS |
|---|---|---|
| January | Brussels sprouts, cabbage, cauliflower, celeriac, celery, leeks, parsnips, seakale, spring greens, swedes, turnips | Early rhubarb. *Imported:* apricots, cranberries |
| February | Brussels sprouts, cabbage, cauliflower, celeriac, celery, leeks, parsnips, seakale, spring greens, swedes | Early rhubarb. *Imported:* apricots |
| March | Broccoli, Brussels sprouts, cabbage, cauliflower, celeriac, celery, leeks, parsnips, seakale, spring greens, swedes | Early rhubarb |
| April | Artichokes (globe), broccoli, Brussels sprouts, leeks, parsnips, spinach, spring greens, swedes | Rhubarb |
| May | Artichokes (globe), asparagus, aubergines, broccoli, cauliflower, courgettes, new carrots, peas, spinach, spring greens, swedes, tomatoes | Rhubarb. *Imported:* apricots |
| June | Artichokes (globe), asparagus, aubergines, beans (broad and French), cauliflower, courgettes, new carrots, new potatoes, peas, spinach, tomatoes. | Cherries, gooseberries, loganberries, peaches, raspberries, rhubarb, strawberries. *Imported:* apricots, bilberries |
| July | Artichokes (globe), asparagus, aubergines, beans (broad, French and runner), cabbage, cauliflower, corn on the cob, courgettes, leeks, new carrots, new potatoes, peas, spinach, tomatoes | Blackcurrants, cherries, gooseberries, loganberries, peaches, plums, raspberries, red currants, strawberries. *Imported:* apricots, bilberries |

*Table 1 – contd*

|  | VEGETABLES | FRUITS |
|---|---|---|
| August | Artichokes (globe), aubergines, beans (French and runner), cabbage, cauliflower, celery, corn on the cob, courgettes, leeks, parsnips, peas, spinach, tomatoes | Apples, blackberries, blackcurrants, cherries, damsons, gooseberries, loganberries, peaches, pears, plums, raspberries, red currants, strawberries. *Imported:* apricots, bilberries |
| September | Artichokes (globe), beans (runner), Brussels sprouts, cabbage, cauliflower, celeriac, celery, courgettes, leeks, parsnips, peas, spinach, swedes | Apples, bilberries, blackberries, damsons, grapes, greengages, pears, plums |
| October | Brussels sprouts, cabbage, celeriac, celery, leeks, parsnips, spinach, swedes, turnips | Apples, blackberries, damsons, grapes, pears |
| November | Brussels sprouts, cabbage, celeriac, celery, leeks, parsnips, spinach, swedes, turnips | Apples, grapes |
| December | Brussels sprouts, cabbage, celeriac, celery, leeks, parsnips, seakale, swedes, turnips | Apples, early rhubarb, grapes. *Imported:* apricots, cranberries |

The seasons given are approximate for vegetables and fruit grown in the U.K. and may vary according to location and local climatic conditions. All vegetables and fruits are at their best for freezing in the early part of their season; for example, peas in May and June and raspberries in June and July.

Home-grown vegetables which are available all the year

round, such as beetroots, carrots, mushrooms and onions, have not been included.

Similarly the imported vegetables and fruits (for example avocado pears, citrus fruits and red and green peppers) have not been shown as they are normally available in most months of the year.

*Table 2   Seasons for fish, meat, poultry and game*

|  | FISH | MEAT AND POULTRY | GAME |
|---|---|---|---|
| January | Cod, haddock, mackerel, oysters, scallops, sole, sprats, turbot, whiting | Goose, turkey | Capercaillie, hare, partridge, pheasant, plover, snipe, wild duck and geese, woodcock |
| February | Mackerel, oysters, salmon, scallops, sprats, turbot, whitebait, whiting | — | Hare |
| March | Mackerel, oysters, salmon, scallops, whitebait | — | — |
| April | Mackerel, mullet (red), prawns, salmon, trout, whitebait | Spring lamb | — |
| May | Crab, herring, mullet (red), plaice, prawns, salmon, trout, whitebait | Spring lamb | — |
| June | Crab, hake, herring, lobster, mullet (red), plaice, prawns, salmon, shrimps, trout, whitebait | — | — |

*Table 2 – contd*

| | FISH | MEAT AND POULTRY | GAME |
|---|---|---|---|
| July | Crab, haddock, hake, halibut, herring, lobster, mullet (grey and red), plaice, prawns, salmon, shrimps, sole, trout | — | — |
| August | Crab, haddock, hake, halibut, herring, lobster, mullet (grey and red), plaice, prawns, salmon, shrimps, sole, trout, turbot | — | Blackcock, grouse, hare, ptarmigan, snipe |
| September | Crab, haddock, hake, halibut, herring, lobster, mullet (grey and red), oysters, plaice, prawns, sole, turbot | Goose, turkey | Blackcock, grouse, hare, partridge, plover, ptarmigan, snipe, wild duck and geese, woodcock (Scotland) |
| October | Cod, haddock, hake, herring, mackerel, mullet (grey), oysters, plaice, scallops, sole, sprats, turbot | Goose, turkey | Blackcock, capercaillie, grouse, hare, partridge, pheasant, plover, ptarmigan, snipe, wild duck and geese, woodcock |
| November | Cod, haddock, hake, herring, mackerel, mullet (grey), oysters, plaice, scallops, sole, sprats, turbot | Goose, turkey | Blackcock, capercaillie, grouse, hare, partridge, pheasant, ptarmigan, plover, snipe, wild duck and geese, woodcock |
| December | Cod, haddock, hake, herring, mackerel, mullet (grey), oysters, plaice, scallops, sole, sprats, turbot, whiting | Goose, turkey | Capercaillie, hare, partridge, pheasant, plover, snipe, wild duck and geese, woodcock |

The fish, meat, poultry and game above have been listed because they have a particular season when they are at their best for freezing. Others, such as beef, pork, veal and chicken, have not been included as they are available all the year round.

# 8

# PACKING FOOD FOR THE FREEZER

Examination of the cartons and wrapping material used by
the commercial producers of quick-frozen food reveals that
a considerable amount of care is taken in selecting the most
suitable type of packaging to ensure that their food reaches
the consumer in top-quality condition. Most of the larger
producers employ specialist packaging engineers who must
not only provide the shape and form of packaging to meet the
sales requirement of the marketing men, but must at the
same time give adequate protection to the food during
freezing, storage and distribution, so as to meet the very
stringent specifications laid down by food technologists and
quality control inspectors.

For home freezing, the merchandising and sales-appeal
requirements of the commercial producer can be ignored,
but use of the correct type of packaging and sealing material
is just as important to ensure a long high-quality storage
life of the food in the freezer. Whatever type of food is being
prepared for freezing, the packaging material must be
capable of preventing dehydration and the consequent loss
of flavour, colour and texture during storage. Because the
low-temperature air in a home freezer is very dry, food will
gradually lose its moisture and develop 'freezer burn'
unless well protected. It is especially important in freezers
fitted with air circulating fans (usually in the larger refriger-
ator/freezer combinations) that care is taken to use only the

best materials and make airtight seals; the circulating low-temperature air will draw moisture much more rapidly from food that is not well protected.

The packaging material and the method of sealing must therefore ensure complete airtightness, be odourless, moisture-proof and vapour-proof at $0°F$ ($-18°C$); at the same time the packaging must be strong enough to withstand handling. The correct type of packaging will also prevent the cross-flavouring of different kinds of foods packed closely together. Many foods, like some game and fish, are liked because of their strong characteristic flavour, while others are chosen for their delicate flavour and texture. Good packaging will prevent 'taste pick-up' between different types of food. Dairy products, cream, and ice cream products contain fat and these pick up other flavours particularly easily.

Airtightness is important to prevent oxygen causing chemical changes in the food. All wrapping material should fit round the food snugly and tightly, so that as much air as possible has been withdrawn before the final permanent seal is made. It is a considerable disappointment and waste of time and money at the outset if high-quality food deteriorates simply because insufficient attention has been paid to packaging or by the use of cheap substitute materials.

The type of packaging material to be used will obviously depend upon the kind and shape of food to be frozen.

## WRAPPING PAPER

Ordinary waxed or greaseproof papers are not recommended for wrapping if the food is to stay in the freezer for longer than a few days. Freezer paper, which has an airtight special coating inside and an uncoated surface outside, which can be labelled, is available in rolls, normally about 18 ins. wide, and supplied in a dispensing box with a metal edge for easy tearing. Freezer paper will resist low temperatures without becoming brittle; it is moisture- and vapour-proof and resistant to fat and grease. After wrapping, as much air as possible should be squeezed out and each fold where air could enter should be sealed with freezer tape.

## POLYTHENE AND CELLOPHANE SHEET

Of the many kinds of polythene and cellophane sheet available, only those recommended for home freezing should be used as these are thicker and moisture- and vapour-proof. Special heat-sealing cellophane is available which can be sealed with the tip of a domestic iron applied directly to the sheet. Polythene is not so easy to heat-seal and tends to stick to the iron unless a strip of paper is placed between sheet and iron. Both types of sheet can be successfully sealed with freezer tape.

## POLYTHENE BAGS

These bags are easy to handle and are particularly suitable for vegetables, small cuts of meat, poultry, game and fish. When they are packed, as much air as possible should be squeezed out and the bag sealed at the top either by heat-sealing – again it is essential that a strip of paper should be placed between polythene and iron – or by freezer tape.

Larger bags can be protected from damage during storage by an overwrap of muslin, brown or greaseproof paper. Similarly, if any food with projecting bones or sharp points is to be frozen it should be covered with muslin or grease-proof paper to ensure that the polythene bag is not punctured. Bags of varying sizes are available, to hold anything from 1 lb. of fruit or vegetables to larger bags for poultry and meat, and specially shaped bags for fish. If using bags for liquid foods, such as sauces, pour through a funnel to ensure that nothing is spilled: the open end must be clean and dry before sealing by heat or with tape. As an alternative to heat-sealing or freezer tape, 'Tite-tie' bag-fasteners can be used, twisted round the neck of the bag.

## WAX CARTONS

Rigid or semi-rigid cartons, as well as being made from mois-ture- and vapour-proof materials, must have closely fitting lids which can be made airtight with freezer tape. There is a wide range of cartons suitable for freezing. Tubs with screw-on tops in varying sizes and cartons with tuck-in lids are the most popular. Shallow waxed cartons with close-fitting lids are suitable for certain types of vegetables – asparagus, broccoli and cauliflower, for example, and smaller joints and cuts of poultry and game, and fish. Rectangular cartons do, of course, make best use of freezer space and will stack well. Since freezer space is valuable, as much food as possible should go into this shape of carton.

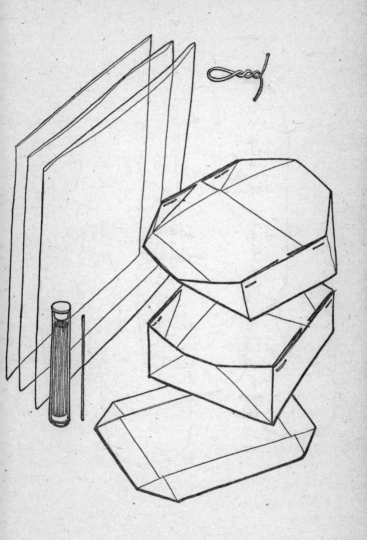

## ALUMINIUM FOIL, TRAYS AND BASINS

Aluminium foil can be used for wrapping most types of food, but should be used in double thickness, with the cut edges folded to make an airtight seal.

Aluminium foil component trays, pie dishes, basins and plates are available in many shapes and sizes. They are particularly useful for prepared entrée dishes and complete meals, also large or individual pies and puddings. They sometimes have waxed paper or aluminium lids which are not particularly easy to seal with tape but, as an alternative, freezer paper, polythene or foil sheet can be used; these are easier to seal.

As well as these types of wrapping material and containers, plastic containers (providing they are odourless), for example Tupperware, can be used. Oven-proof and flame-proof dishes such as Pyrosil are also suitable, but their use may be rather impracticable for long-storage periods. A more economical and convenient method is to line the dish with foil or polythene sheet, place the food inside and fold or gather the top together, make an airtight seal with tape or bag fasteners, and put the complete dish into the freezer. After the food has frozen the wrapped food can be lifted out of the dish and stored. The dish can then be returned for kitchen use. When food packed in this way is wanted, it can be unwrapped, placed in the same type of dish in which it was frozen, and put in the oven to heat through.

Most containers can be used more than once, provided they are carefully washed, dried and kept clean before using again. Spare lids of the screw-on or insert-fitting type can often be bought separately if the originals have been damaged from first use.

It is a good idea to keep odd pieces of polythene sheet and freezer paper, as these can be used to separate portions of food packed in the same bag or container. Fish, chops, steaks and other individual portions of food can be packed in layers with two thicknesses of moisture-vapour-proof material between each layer. This interleaving is especially useful if a particular number of portions are to be packed and frozen in one single container. This means that single portions can be taken from the bulk pack without thawing out the entire package.

## LABELLING AND MARKING

Each package of food should ideally be marked with details of its contents and the date of freezing. For those foods which have a particularly short storage life, it may also be helpful to mark the latest date by which the food should be used in order to enjoy it at its best. Cooked dishes should also be clearly marked with the name of the dish, the number of portions, and the date. A chinagraph pencil or a felt-tipped pen is useful for marking paper-wrapped packages and cartons. Small labels which can be secured with bag fasteners or freezer tape can be used for polythene bags and cartons. Adhesive labels which will not lose their adhesion at low temperature are also available. Different coloured felt-tipped pens or labels may also be helpful in quickly identifying different types of food, for example red for meat and meat dishes, blue for fish, green for vegetables, etc.

*Table 3   Quick guide to packaging material*

| Material used: | Recommended for: | Points to note: |
|---|---|---|
| Moisture-vapour-proof paper | Cuts of meat, poultry, game, pies, cakes, flans, uncooked pastry, bread and rolls | Special sealing tape required. Sharp corners, e.g. bones of meat, should be protected in muslin or greaseproof to prevent puncturing the paper |
| Polythene sheets Cellophane sheets | As above | Require bag fasteners or sealing tape. More pliable than paper. Useful for interleaving between layers of food |
| Polythene bags | Vegetables, fruit, meat, poultry, game and fish | Available in many sizes ranging from 1 lb. suitable for vegetables, to very large ones for whole salmon, etc. Fastening by bag fasteners or heat-sealing (an ordinary household iron can be used at the temperature for ironing rayon (240° F) or a special heat-sealing iron can now be purchased, which reduces any risk of burning the polythene) |
| Waxed boxes, tubs and cartons | Soups, sauces, fish, chops, steaks, vegetables and prepared meals | These have airtight lids. Stack on top of each other. Can be used again after washing and drying carefully. Available in wide range of sizes |
| Aluminium foil sheet | Almost all food, especially irregular shapes, e.g. poultry, game, cuts of meat, etc. Lining of casserole dishes | Use double thickness, fold cut edges to make airtight seal |
| Foil trays, plates and basins | Prepared meals, individual portions, pies, etc. | Available in varying sizes. Useful for portion control (e.g. 2-, 4- or 6-portion sizes). Can be used again. The top should be covered with freezer paper or polythene, and sealed with sealing tape |

As well as marking the packs it is helpful to keep an inventory of the type of food, the number and weight of the packs, and the date. Every time food is taken from the freezer, delete it from the inventory. This provides an easy method of checking stock and also ensures that the food which has been in the longest is used first.

Most large stationers and department stores nowadays sell some, if not all, of the special packing material mentioned, though it may not be easy, particularly for those living away from towns, to find a source of supply of certain sizes or types of containers.

The following suppliers of packaging materials will send a list on request and will also send supplies by post:

Frigicold Ltd,
166 Dukes Road,
Acton,
London, W3 OTJ.

Harrods Ltd,
Knightsbridge,
London, SW1.

John Lewis,
Oxford Street,
London, W1.

Lakeland Plastics
(Windermere) Ltd,
Alexandra Road,
Windermere.

# PREPARING FOOD FOR FREEZING

It is easy to freeze food even without any previous experience. Follow the simple rules and there need be no failures. Detailed recommendations are given for each food group – vegetables, fruit, fish, meat, poultry, game and dairy products. The fundamental principles which will lead to successful freezing of all foods are:

Freeze only young fresh vegetables and fruit, really fresh sea or river fish, and best-quality meat and poultry.

Prepare the food correctly – i.e. blanch vegetables, select and wash fruit, prepare and clean poultry and fish. Pack the food correctly, exclude as much air as possible, then seal and label each pack.

Freeze small quantities of food at a time so that the temperature of the freezer does not rise above 0°F ( −18°C) (see Chapter 7, p. 55).

Finally, ensure good stock rotation on the basis of 'first in and first out' to ensure the best flavour and quality of food from the freezer.

## VEGETABLES

Ideally vegetables for the freezer should be prepared and put into the freezer within 2–3 hours of picking. If this is not always possible, particularly for the town dweller who has to rely on the market or shop, make sure that the vegetables are as young and fresh as possible. Buying straight from the market or a reputable shop is best. The country dweller will have an abundant supply, and here the rule is not to pick too much at once. While preparing small quantities, keep any excess in the refrigerator, as vegetables rapidly lose freshness and food value if allowed to stand in a warm room.

## Selection of vegetables

Freezing does not improve the quality of the original product; what goes into the freezer will be the same when it comes out – therefore the fresher the vegetables, the better. As well as being fresh, the vegetables should be young and tender – once past their peak of maturity they tend to be drier and tougher, and freezing will not improve this.

## Vegetables suitable for freezing

Most vegetables can be frozen but some more successfully than others. Those with a high water content, such as lettuce, cucumber and other salad vegetables, are not really suitable as they become limp and lose their texture when thawed. Tomatoes and onions can be frozen but are then only good for cooking, as they lose their crispness after freezing. But they are excellent for sauces, soups and casseroles, and their fresh flavour is retained. A general guide is that the vegetables which are cooked before eating can be frozen successfully.

## Preparation

Vegetables should be selected and prepared, peas and broad beans podded, carrots peeled and washed, as if for immediate cooking. Leafy vegetables such as Brussels sprouts and cauliflowers need to be soaked for $\frac{1}{2}$ hour in cold salted water (3 teaspoons to 1 pint) to remove insects. All vegetables must be blanched (scalded) in boiling water for a few minutes to stop the growth of enzymes, otherwise the quality, flavour and storage life deteriorate in the freezer.

## Blanching

Market gardeners and home growers of vegetables will have noticed that vegetables which have not been harvested before a severe frost lose colour and flavour when they are eventually picked and may be bitter and unpleasant in taste after cooking. The loss of flavour is due to increased enzymic activity, which is a natural deterioration in all foods and is caused, in this case, by slow freezing, eventual thawing and late harvesting. It is for this reason that it is inadvisable to home-freeze raw vegetables without first preparing them for cooking, and then blanching them in boiling water for the recommended time. Blanching inactivates the enzymes and stops the development of off-flavours. It also prevents the deterioration of vegetables after harvesting by stopping respiration and considerably retards the loss of vitamins during subsequent storage.

Blanching can be done either by immersing the vegetables in boiling water and scalding for the required time, or by steaming. The former is the simplest method unless a large steamer is available, but steam blanching causes smaller losses of vitamins than hot-water treatment. The only equipment necessary is a large saucepan (8-pint) and a wire basket which will fit into the saucepan. It is advisable to blanch small quantities at a time, either ½ lb. or 1 lb., otherwise the water takes a long time to return to the boil, making it a lengthy process.

A basin with chilled water to cool the vegetables before drying and packing should also be available.

Have all the equipment ready before starting, and the job will be much easier and quicker if it can be done on a 'production-line' basis.

1. Prepare the vegetables according to type.

2. Weigh out and put ½ lb. or 1 lb. into the wire basket.

3. Plunge the basket into boiling water and start the blanching time from when the water returns to the boil.

4. Remove the basket of vegetables and plunge it into chilled water.

5. Drain off excess liquid and dry as much as possible. Pack as suggested.

### Packaging

All vegetables can be packed in wax cartons or polythene bags. The type of vegetable, the weight and the date should be marked on each package.

### Cooking frozen vegetables

Frozen vegetables require shorter cooking time as they have already been blanched. For best results, good texture and flavour, cook them while still frozen in the minimum amount of boiling salted water. They need only ½–⅔ of the time required for market-bought vegetables.

Table 4  *Vegetables*

| | PREPARATION | BLANCHING TIME, MINUTES | PACKAGING | HIGH QUALITY STORAGE LIFE, MONTHS |
|---|---|---|---|---|
| Artichokes (globe) | Remove coarse outer leaves and scrape and trim stalks and tips of leaves. To prevent discoloration, add ¼ pint of lemon juice to 4 pints of boiling water when blanching | 7 | Chill, drain and dry. Pack in wax cartons | 9–12 |
| Asparagus | Select stalks according to thickness. Wash and scrape stalks and trim to equal lengths | 2–4 depending on thickness | Chill, drain and dry. Pack in wax cartons, alternating tip and stalk ends | 9–12 |
| Aubergines | Cut into ½ in. slices. Put into salted water (3 teaspoons to 1 pint) to prevent discoloration before blanching | 4 | Chill, drain and dry. Pack in layers with greaseproof paper between, in wax cartons | 9–12 |
| Beans (broad) | Pod and discard blemished beans | 3 | Chill, drain and dry. Pack in wax cartons or polythene bags | 9–12 |

*Table 4 – contd*

| | PREPARATION | BLANCHING TIME, MINUTES | PACKAGING | HIGH QUALITY STORAGE MONTHS |
|---|---|---|---|---|
| **Beans** (French or runner) | Wash and trim ends. Leave whole or slice | Whole: 4 Sliced: 3 | Chill, drain and dry. Pack in wax cartons or polythene bags | 9–12 |
| **Beetroot** | Best to freeze young small beets. Leave whole and cook until tender. Rub off skins | None | Chill, drain and dry. Pack in wax cartons | 6 |
| **Broccoli** | Wash, clean and trim stalks to equal length | 3–4 depending on thickness | Chill, drain and dry. Pack in wax cartons | 9–12 |
| **Brussels sprouts** | Trim and remove discoloured leaves and cross-cut the stalks. Soak in salted water | 3–5 depending on size | Chill, drain and dry. Pack in wax cartons or polythene bags | 9–12 |
| **Cabbage** (including spring greens) | Trim off coarse outer leaves. Wash in salted water and cut or tear into shreds | 2 | Chill, drain and dry. Pack in wax cartons or polythene bags | 6 |
| **Carrots** | Remove tops, wash and scrape. Leave small new carrots whole | Whole: 5 Sliced: 3 | Chill, drain and dry. Pack in wax cartons or polythene bags | 6–8 |

| Cauliflower | Remove outer leaves and separate into sprigs. Soak in cold salted water | 4 | Chill, drain and dry. Pack in wax cartons or polythene bags | 6-8 |
|---|---|---|---|---|
| Celeriac | Wash, trim and scrape. Cut into slices | 3 | Chill, drain and dry. Pack in wax cartons or polythene bags | 9-12 |
| Celery | Remove coarse outer stalks if blemished. Trim stalks and cut into 2 to 3-in. lengths. The hearts can be frozen whole if preferred | 3-4 (longer time for hearts) | Chill, drain and dry Pack in wax cartons or polythene bags | 9-12 |
| Corn on the cob | Remove outer husks, trim ends and wash | Small: 7 Large: 10 | Chill, drain and dry. Pack in wax cartons | 9-12 |
| Corn kernels | Remove outer husks. Scrape kernels off the cob | 5 | Chill, drain and dry. Pack in wax cartons or polythene bags | 9-12 |
| Courgettes | Wash and cut into slices | 3 | Chill, drain and dry. Pack in layers with grease-proof paper between, in wax cartons | 9-12 |
| Leeks | Remove coarse outer leaves and trim ends. Wash well under running water. Leave whole or slice | 2-4 depending on size | Chill, drain and dry. Pack in wax cartons or polythene bags | 6 |

*Table 4 – contd*

| | PREPARATION | BLANCHING TIME, MINUTES | PACKAGING | HIGH QUALITY STORAGE LIFE, MONTHS |
|---|---|---|---|---|
| Mushrooms | Wash and peel field ones. Wash cultivated ones and trim stalks. Leave whole or slice. Put into lemon juice and water (3 teaspoons to 1 pint cold water) to prevent discoloration | Whole: 4 Sliced: 2 | Chill, drain and dry. Pack in wax cartons | 9–12 |
| Onions | Although these lose crispness after freezing, they retain their flavour and are good for cooking. Peel and slice | 2 | Pack in small quantities ready for use in wax cartons | 2–3 |
| New potatoes | Will lose texture after freezing. Select potatoes of a similar size. Scrape and wash | 4 | Chill, drain and dry. Pack in wax cartons or polythene bags | 9–12 |
| Parsnips | Scrape and wash. Cut into lengths or slices | 3 | Chill, drain and dry. Pack in wax cartons or polythene bags | 9–12 |

| | | | |
|---|---|---|---|
| Peas | Pod and discard any blemished peas | 1½ | Chill, drain and dry. Pack in wax cartons or polythene bags |
| Peppers (red and green) | Wash, remove seeds and halve or slice | 2 | Chill, drain and dry. Pack in wax cartons or polythene bags |
| Spinach and seakale | Remove coarse outer leaves. Wash in cold salted water | 2 | Chill, drain and dry. Pack in wax cartons or polythene bags |
| Tomatoes | These become soft after freezing but are good for cooking. Remove skin. Leave whole or slice or quarter | None | Pack in wax cartons |
| Turnips and swedes | Remove thick peel. Cut into 1-in. cubes | 3 | Chill, drain and dry. Pack into wax cartons or polythene bags |
| Herbs: e.g., Marjoram, Mint. Parsley, Rosemary, Sage, Thyme | Wash, drain and dry. Chop finely. May lose colour and flavour during storage | 1 | Wrap in small quantities required for use in pieces of foil. Put foil packages in polythene bags, using a separate one for each herb |
| | | | *N.B.* When packing vegetables in wax cartons leave ½ in. headspace to allow for expansion |

9–12
9–12
9–12
9–12
9–12
6–8

FRUIT

It is even more important to freeze fruit, particularly soft fruit, at the peak of its maturity before it becomes over-ripe and soft. Fruit is very easy to prepare for the freezer and is well worth freezing, particularly fruit that has a short season, such as raspberries, strawberries and currants, all of which have a fairly long high-quality storage life.

To maintain the high-quality storage life and colour of fruit it is better to pack most fruit in dry sugar or a syrup solution. Some fruits are best frozen in syrup and others in dry sugar, but this is just to make them look better when they are thawed.

The best way to pack depends on how the fruit is to be used. A syrup is advisable if the fruit is to be served uncooked – the exception being raspberries and strawberries, as they contain natural juice – but a dry pack is better if the fruit is to be baked in pies and puddings. Some fruit – gooseberries and apples, for example – can be frozen with no sugar at all, but the storage life will be slightly shorter.

*Darkening of fruit*

Light-coloured fruits such as pears and peaches darken quickly unless put into a syrup solution immediately after peeling and cutting and even so they may discolour slightly. Colour is retained by adding ascorbic acid (vitamin C) to the pack. Commercial ascorbic-acid tablets can be bought in chemists. They are available in different strengths, but the 500 mgm tablets are probably the most convenient. Dissolve a tablet in a teaspoon of cold water and add this to each pint of cold sugar syrup. Do not mix in iron or copper pans.

If the fruit is to be packed dry, dip it in ascorbic-acid solution (500 mgm tablet to 1 pint cold water) before drying and packing it with sugar.

## Preparation of fruit

All fruit should be selected, and soft or mushy fruits discarded. Clean, wash and prepare firm fruit as if for serving. Fruits with stones, such as plums and cherries, may be left whole or stoned if preferred. Prepare only as much fruit as can easily be handled at a time – usually 5 or 6 containers. Any unprepared fruit should be kept in a refrigerator or cool place until it can be prepared and packed.

## Packaging

Firm fruits, such as apples, pineapple and plums, can be packed in polythene bags with dry sugar. Wax cartons are better for soft fruits, to prevent bruising, and for fruits packed with a syrup solution.

To make cooking, serving and stock control easy, pack the fruit in quantities to suit meal requirements, for example, in $\frac{1}{2}$ lb. or 1 lb. containers. If fruit is to be frozen for jam making later, it can be packed in larger polythene bags or wax cartons.

Dry sugar pack: After washing and drying the fruit, if light-coloured fruit dip in ascorbic-acid solution, pack into cartons or polythene bags and sprinkle with sugar; $\frac{1}{4}$ lb. sugar to each pound of fruit is generally sufficient, but more can be added if the fruit is preferred sweeter. Alternatively, more sugar can be added before serving when the fruit is thawing.

Syrup solution pack: Make up a quantity of syrup before preparing the fruit. The syrup should be cooled and preferably chilled before use. Allow $\frac{1}{3}$ pint syrup to each pound of fruit. The sweetness of the syrup depends upon the tartness of the fruit and on individual taste, but a general guide is given with the packaging recommendations for individual fruits.

Syrup solutions:

30 per cent  $8\frac{1}{2}$ oz. sugar to 1 pint of water.

40 per cent  13 oz. sugar to 1 pint of water.

50 per cent  20 oz. sugar to 1 pint of water.

Add the sugar to the water, bring to the boil and simmer until the sugar is dissolved. Cover and allow to cool or chill before use.

When packing fruit, leave at least $\frac{1}{2}$ in. headspace at the top of the carton or bag, as fruit juices expand during freezing.

Seal the pack, label it with the name of the fruit, the amount of sugar, the weight and the date.

To ensure that the dry sugar or syrup thoroughly penetrates the fruit before freezing (this reduces oxidation and enzyme action during storage and thawing) leave the package of fruit in a cool place, preferably in the refrigerator, for about an hour before freezing.

*Cooked fruit*

Fruit which has been cooked can be frozen, and this is particularly useful when it is to be used in a sauce, a pudding or as an accompaniment to a dish.

Small quantities of fresh apple purée or cranberry sauce, for example, can be taken from the freezer when needed.

The fruit should be prepared, cooked and packed in small cartons or polythene bags (leaving headspace for expansion) to suit the amount required for a meal.

*Table 5    Fruit*

| | PREPARATION | PACKAGING | HIGH QUALITY STORAGE LIFE, MONTHS |
|---|---|---|---|
| Apples | Use good varieties when just ripe and crisp. Peel, core and slice. Blanch for 2 minutes if no sugar used | Pack in dry sugar or 40 per cent syrup with ascorbic-acid solution | 9–12 |
| Apple purée | Peel, core and slice. Cook until tender and sieve; sweeten if liked | Pack in wax cartons and seal | 9 |
| Apricots | Can be frozen in halves, or peeled and sliced | 40 per cent syrup or dry pack. Add ascorbic-acid solution to pack | 9–12 |
| Avocado pears | Best frozen as purée. Not very satisfactory whole or sliced. Peel, remove stone and mash | Add 1 teaspoon lemon juice to 1 pint of purée. Mix with salt and pepper or sugar. Pack in wax tubs and seal | 2 |
| Bilberries | Pick firm fruit. Remove stalks. Wash and dry | Cover with dry sugar, ¼ lb. sugar to 1 lb. fruit | 9–12 |
| Blackberries | Pick firm berries. Remove stalks. Wash and dry | As Bilberries | 9–12 |
| Blackcurrants | Strip currants off stem. Wash and dry | With dry sugar or 50 per cent syrup | 9–12 |

*Table 5 – contd*

| | PREPARATION | PACKAGING | HIGH QUALITY STORAGE LIFE, MONTHS |
|---|---|---|---|
| Citrus fruits, lemons, oranges, grapefruit, etc. | Peel and remove pith and pips. Slice or segment or squeeze for juice | Pack in 30 per cent syrup. For juice – add sugar to taste | 9–12 |
| Cherries | Wash and stone if liked | In dry sugar or 30 per cent syrup | 9–12 |
| Cranberries | Wash. Freeze whole or cook and sieve for purée | Pack whole in dry sugar or 50 per cent syrup. Purée; add sugar to taste | 9–12 |
| Damsons | Wash and stone if liked | Can be packed with or without sugar. With sugar, use dry sugar pack | 9–12 |
| Greengages | Wash, halve and remove stones | Pack in cartons with 50 per cent syrup | 9–12 |
| Gooseberries | Top and tail. Wash and dry | Can be packed without sugar. Dry sugar – allow $\frac{1}{4}$ lb. sugar to 1 lb. fruit; or in 50 per cent syrup | 9–12 |
| Grapes | Wash and dry. Halve and remove seeds | Pack in 30 per cent syrup | 9–12 |
| Loganberries | Select firm berries | Dry sugar pack – allow $\frac{1}{4}$ lb. to 1 lb. of fruit | 9–12 |
| Melon | Peel, remove seeds and cut into slices or cubes | Sprinkle with lemon juice. Pack in dry sugar, $\frac{1}{4}$ lb. to 1 lb. fruit, or 30 per cent syrup | 9–12 |

| | PREPARATION | PACKAGING | HIGH QUALITY STORAGE LIFE, MONTHS |
|---|---|---|---|
| Peaches | Peel and slice. Avoid handling too much | Pack in 50 per cent syrup with ascorbic-acid solution | 9–12 |
| Pears | Peel, core and quarter or slice. Pack immediately or sprinkle lemon juice over to keep white | Pack in 30 per cent syrup with ascorbic-acid solution | 9–12 |
| Pineapple | Peel and core. Cut into slices or cubes | Pack in 50 per cent syrup | 9–12 |
| Plums | Wash, halve and remove stones | Pack in dry sugar, $\frac{1}{4}$ lb. – 1 lb. fruit or 50 per cent syrup | 9–12 |
| Raspberries | Select firm berries | Pack in dry sugar, $\frac{1}{4}$ lb. to 1 lb. fruit | 9–12 |
| Redcurrants | Strip off stem. Wash and dry | Pack in dry sugar, $\frac{1}{4}$ lb. to 1 lb. fruit | 9–12 |
| Rhubarb | Freeze young tender stalks. Wash and cut into 1 in. pieces | Pack in dry sugar. $\frac{1}{4}$ lb. to $\frac{1}{2}$ lb. to 1 lb. fruit, or 50 per cent syrup. Can be packed already cooked and sweetened | 9–12 |
| Strawberries | Select firm berries. Wash and hull. Leave whole or halve | Pack in dry sugar, $\frac{1}{4}$ lb. to 1 lb. fruit  *N.B.* When packing fruit in wax cartons leave $\frac{1}{2}$–$\frac{3}{4}$ in. headspace to allow for expansion | 9–12 |

FISH

Fish should ideally be frozen within hours of it being caught and cleaned. Like this, it will have a longer high-quality storage life and retain its flavour and quality. Unless it is possible to obtain really fresh fish it is not really worth freezing it except for short-time storage for a special occasion.

If supplies of fresh fish are available at the coast or local rivers, there is no problem. Alternatively, rely on a reputable fishmonger who will appreciate the problem and will try to supply fish that has just been received, packed in ice.

*Preparation of fish*

Fish should be prepared for freezing as for cooking – that is, cleaned, gutted, the head, tail and fins removed and the scales scraped. Large fish is easier to pack and freeze if it is first cut into steaks or filleted, although it can be frozen whole if space allows; this is obviously impractical unless the whole fish is to be cooked and used at one time. Smaller fish that are usually served whole, for example Dover sole, herring and trout, can be frozen whole.

There are three types of fish and each requires different preparation before freezing. The high-quality storage life varies significantly with each type of fish. The three types are white, oily and shell fish.

White fish has, on the whole, a reasonably long high-quality storage life – 6–9 months, depending on the condition and freshness at the time of freezing. In order to retain the firm texture of white fish it may help to dip individual steaks or fillets in a brine solution (2 oz. salt to 1 pint cold water) for 30 seconds before packing, but the storage life is halved; otherwise pack dry.

Oily fish, on the other hand, because of its higher fat content, has a shorter storage life than white fish – 4–6 months. This type of fish is well worth freezing, especially if you can obtain it in a really fresh condition and particularly such fish as salmon and trout, which have limited availability.

Shell fish, by comparison, have a relatively short storage life, and therefore it is only worth while packing and freezing quantities which will be used within the maximum storage period.

*Crabs and lobsters* Ideally crabs and lobsters should be bought alive and cooked by plunging them into boiling water for 10–15 minutes. Some high-class fishmongers will prepare crabs and lobsters, in which case these should be collected while still warm. As soon as they have cooled, remove the meat from the shell and claws and pack it into wax cartons or in aluminium foil containers.

*Oysters and scallops* These are best frozen uncooked, but must first be removed from their shells. After opening the shells carefully, remove the fish and retain the natural juices. Pack the fish into wax cartons or foil containers and cover with the natural juices. If this is not sufficient to cover, add brine solution made up from 1 tablespoon salt to 1 quart of water, leaving 1 in. headspace. To prevent the fish from rising in the carton, cover with crumpled greaseproof paper before fitting the lid and sealing.

*Prawns and shrimps* These can be frozen cooked or uncooked, but to achieve the longest storage life they are better uncooked. Cooking before freezing tends to toughen the flesh during storage. The shells of uncooked prawns and shrimps may be left on, but the heads and tails should be removed. They should be thoroughly washed in cold salted water before packing in wax cartons or polythene bags.

## Packaging

All fish should be well packed before freezing, not only to prevent any tendency to dry out but also to prevent fish flavours being transferred to other foods in the freezer.

Whole small fish and fillets or steaks cut from larger fish should be tightly wrapped in moisture-vapour-proof paper or foil, excluding as much air as possible, and then sealed with freezer tape. They can then be packed into wax cartons or polythene bags. This allows the fish to be taken out in quantities as required for use. Alternatively, fish fillets can be packed in layers in wax cartons with a double layer of moisture-vapour-proof paper between each layer. If this method is used the carton must be sealed with freezer tape.

Whole large fish, like salmon, should be wrapped in moisture-vapour-proof paper or foil, excluding as much air as possible before sealing with freezer tape, and then placed in a large polythene bag.

## Cooking

Small fish and fillets and steaks of larger fish can be cooked while still frozen, but they will require longer cooking time.

Allow a $\frac{1}{4}$ to $\frac{1}{2}$ longer cooking time than usual. If the fish is
going to be fried or grilled, use a medium heat to avoid over-
cooking of the outside before the centre is cooked through;
this especially applies to thick pieces of fish. If the fish is to
be coated with egg and breadcrumbs or batter, or is to
be stuffed or fried in deep fat it is better to let it thaw out
slightly.

Leave whole large fish, e.g. salmon, to thaw completely
before cooking, otherwise it is very difficult to cook through
evenly. The best way of thawing it is to transfer the fish, in
its wrapping, to the refrigerator or a cool place 12–24 hours
before cooking.

*Table 6   Fish*

| | PREPARATION | PACKAGING | HIGH QUALITY STORAGE LIFE, MONTHS |
|---|---|---|---|
| **White fish**<br>Cod<br>Haddock<br>Plaice<br>Sole<br>Whiting | Remove head, tail, scales and fins, and gut the fish. Wash in cold water. If liked, the skin can be removed. Small fish, plaice, sole, etc., can be frozen whole or in fillets. Cut large fish into steaks or fillets | Dip in brine solution (2 oz. salt to 1 pint cold water) for 30 seconds. Drain well and wrap whole small fish or pieces in moisture-vapour-proof paper. Pack in flat wax cartons or wrap in polythene or foil sheet | 6–9 |

*Table 6 – contd*

| | PREPARATION | PACKAGING | HIGH QUALITY STORAGE LIFE, MONTHS |
|---|---|---|---|
| *Oily fish*<br>Halibut<br>Herring<br>Mackerel<br>Mullet<br>Salmon<br>Turbot<br>Trout | Remove head, tail, scales and fins, and gut the fish. Wash in cold water. Small fish, herring, mackerel, mullet and trout can be frozen whole. Cut large fish into steaks or fillets | Wrap each fish or piece of fish in moisture-vapour-proof paper. Pack in flat wax cartons or wrap in polythene or foil sheet | 4 |
| *Shellfish*<br>Crab<br>Lobster | Cook before preparing for freezing. Remove the meat from the shells | Pack in wax cartons. Leave 1 in. headspace and cover | 3 |
| Oysters<br>Scallops | Wash well in cold salted water to remove sand and grit. Remove from the shells and preserve the liquor | Pack in wax or foil cartons, cover with liquor mixed with brine solution. Leave 1 in. headspace and cover | 3 |
| Prawns<br>Shrimps | Can be frozen cooked or uncooked. Cooked: Wash well. Boil in salted water for 8–10 minutes. Leave to cool and remove heads, tails, shells and veins. Uncooked: Remove heads and tails, wash well and drain. (Remove shells and veins after thawing.) | Pack in polythene bags or wax cartons | Cooked: 1–2 Uncooked: 3 |

MEAT

It is an advantage to have a selection of meat in the freezer
for different occasions and meals. Joints of meat, chops,
meat for stewing, all provide a good basic supply. Butchers
will sell cuts of meat as requested and many of them will
advise on the best buy for the time of year. The professional
butcher can be relied on to dress and hang carcasses before
jointing. It is obviously economical to buy when market
prices are low and it may also be more economical to buy in
bulk, though this will depend on the size of the freezer and the
space available.

Some stores will supply sides or cuts of meat for
freezing for dispatch to all parts of the country, and these
are prepared, wrapped and labelled ready for the
freezer.

*Packaging*

Airtight wrapping for meat is very important, otherwise,
after a time, the meat will become dry (often known as
'freezer burn') and will be tough. Wrap meat in cuts and
joints that will be convenient when required for cooking and
serving. Small cuts, such as steaks and chops, can be individually wrapped or packed in fours or sixes in a flat wax
carton with a layer of foil, waxed or moisture-vapour-proof
paper between each piece.

Remove bones as far as practicable from joints of meat, as
it is waste of freezer space to leave them in. This also makes
the joint easier to wrap. The bones which have been removed
can be made into stock, cooled and frozen in wax cartons,

and then used in soups, stews and sauces. Freeze stock in ½-pint or 1-pint cartons for easy use.

## Cooking

Meat can be cooked while still frozen, but for more even cooking large joints should be thawed out, preferably overnight, in the main body of the refrigerator. Small cuts will only take an hour or so to thaw, but can be cooked while frozen, allowing slightly longer than the usual cooking time. Do not leave meat too long in the thawed state before cooking it, otherwise the natural juices will start to drip.

## Cooked meat

Meat that has been cooked, either roasted, casseroled, or made into other dishes, can be frozen. The high-quality storage life is not as long as for uncooked meats, but it is possible to save a lot of time if some cooked meat dishes are in the freezer ready for heating and serving. (See 'Cooking for the Freezer', Chapter 10).

## Bacon and ham

Because these have already been preserved by curing they are best kept in a refrigerator. In a freezer the salting will cause rancidity in a very short time which will make it unpalatable.

*Table 7    Meat*

|  | PREPARATION | PACKAGING | HIGH QUALITY STORAGE LIFE, MONTHS |
|---|---|---|---|
| **Beef** | | | |
| Large cuts | Remove bones and excess fat | Wrap in moisture-vapour-proof paper. Seal | 10–12 |
| Small cuts | Trim bones and fat | Wrap in moisture-vapour-proof paper, polythene or wax cartons with layers of paper between | 6–8 |
| **Lamb** | | | |
| Large cuts | As above | Wrap in moisture-vapour-proof paper. Seal | 10–12 |
| Small cuts | As above | Wrap in moisture-vapour-proof paper, polythene or wax cartons with layers of paper between | 6–8 |
| **Pork** | | | |
| Large cuts | As above | Wrap in moisture-vapour-proof paper. Seal | 4–5 |
| Small cuts | As above | Wrap in moisture-vapour-proof paper, polythene or wax cartons with layers of paper between | 3–4 |
| **Veal** | | | |
| Large cuts | As above | Wrap in moisture-vapour-proof paper. Seal | 4–5 |

*Table 7 – contd*

|  | PREPARATION | PACKAGING | HIGH QUALITY STORAGE LIFE, MONTHS |
|---|---|---|---|
| Small cuts | As above | Wrap in moisture-vapour-proof paper, polythene or wax cartons with layers of paper between | 3–4 |
| Offal | Clean, trim and remove excess fat | Wrap in moisture-vapour-proof paper | 2–3 |
| Mince meat | Only freeze if freshly minced | Pack in wax cartons and seal | 1–2 |
| Sausages | If home-made, omit salt as this accelerates rancidity of meat | Pack in wax cartons or polythene bags | 1–2 |

## POULTRY AND GAME

Chicken, duck, turkey, goose and game can all be success-fully frozen and stored in the freezer, provided the best-quality birds are selected. They should be in a prime healthy condition; young, plump birds are better to freeze than older, tougher ones. Poultry can be frozen either whole or cut into quarters or joints.

*Preparation of uncooked poultry*

Preferably, the birds should be starved for 24 hours

before killing. They should then be well bled (which is essential for good preservation), before being plucked, drawn, and cleaned.

When plucking, remove all the hairs and feathers and cut off the head and feet. All the internal organs should be removed including the vent, crop and windpipe, and the inside carefully washed out in cold water. If there is a lot of excess fat on the bird, remove as much as possible, as it might become rancid and spoil the whole bird.

The liver and giblets can be retained, and after cleaning and washing should be wrapped in polythene. Before wrapping for freezing, leave poultry in the refrigerator overnight; if birds are not chilled before freezing they are inclined to be tough.

## Joints or quarters

The prepared and cleaned birds can be jointed, or cut into quarters, so that they are ready to use for casseroles, grilling or frying. Small pieces are useful, as they can be taken from the freezer if individual portions are required.

## Packaging

*Whole birds* Truss and tie whole birds as for cooking. The washed giblets can be wrapped in polythene and put inside the bird, or else frozen separately. The latter is advisable if the storage period is to be longer than 3 months.

It is not advisable to stuff birds before freezing. The stuffing slows the rate of freezing and will become moist and may develop 'off-flavours'.

T–D

Wrap the bird in moisture-vapour-proof paper or polythene bags. Protect any sharp points with muslin, to prevent the paper being punctured.

*Joints or quarters* These can be wrapped individually, or several pieces packed in a wax carton. If packing in a carton, place a double layer of paper between the pieces so that they can be separated easily. Label each carton with the number of pieces.

After freezing, the bones of poultry may turn dark. This is quite natural and occurs when the blood cells of the bone marrow start to seep through. It has no effect on flavour.

## Cooking

For even cooking, it is better to leave poultry to thaw right through before cooking. This particularly applies to whole birds, as it takes time for the heat to penetrate. Leave whole birds to thaw overnight or longer in the main body of the refrigerator. Smaller pieces can be cooked while frozen.

*Game birds* The same rules apply to game birds as to poultry, when they are in season (see chart p. 59). The best results are obtained if the birds are bled as soon after shooting as possible, and a period of time should be allowed for hanging.

Game birds should be hung in order for the full flavour to develop, otherwise they have a bland taste, similar to poultry. The length of time really depends on personal taste and the type and age of the bird, but generally partridge, pheasant and snipe require longer hanging than other game birds. After a few days, the tail feathers can be plucked easily, and then the birds are ready for freezing.

*Table 8   Poultry and Game*

| | PREPARATION | PACKAGING | HIGH QUALITY STORAGE LIFE, MONTHS |
|---|---|---|---|
| **Poultry** | | | |
| Chicken Duck Goose Turkey | Remove head, tail and feathers. Clean and truss. Pack whole or divide into joints or quarters | Wrap tightly in moisture-vapour-proof paper, foil or put into polythene bags. Seal with tape or bag ties for the latter<br>Joints or quarters can be wrapped individually or packed in wax cartons with a layer of paper between each one | 9–12<br>6<br>6<br>6 |
| Liver and giblets | Wash in cold water | Pack in wax cartons or polythene bags | 2–3 |
| **Game** | | | |
| Blackcock Capercaillie Grouse Partridge Pheasant Plover Quail Wild duck | After bleeding, hang for the specified time or slightly less, according to personal taste. Pluck, draw and clean | Wrap in moisture-vapour-proof paper, double polythene or foil. Seal with tape | 6–8 |
| Woodcock | Not usually drawn, but remove head, legs and feathers | | |
| Hare Rabbit | Remove heads and bleed. Hang hares in cool, airy place for 48 hours. Skin and wash hare and rabbit well. Divide into joints | Wrap individually in moisture-vapour-proof paper, double polythene or foil. Or pack in wax cartons with a layer of paper between each joint | 4–6 |

DAIRY FOODS

Eggs, butter, cheese and cream are readily available these days, and it seems a waste of freezer space to store large quantities, but a few packages of each do provide an emergency supply.

Eggs selected for freezing should be new-laid and clean. They do not freeze well in their shells as they will probably crack, and without preparation the yolks will toughen and will subsequently not mix with the whites. For short-time storage eggs can be broken and put into individual containers.

For whole eggs it is best to mix the yolks and whites together gently, adding $\frac{1}{2}$ teaspoon of salt or $\frac{1}{2}$ tablespoon of sugar to 6 eggs. Pack the mixed eggs in usable quantities, i.e. 4, 6 or 8 eggs in wax cartons. It is obviously important to label each pack with the number of eggs and the type of seasoning used so that the sweetened eggs are used in puddings and cakes and the salted ones in savoury dishes. If large quantities are packed and only a small amount is required, about 2 tablespoonfuls is equivalent to one egg in the shell.

Alternatively yolks and whites can be frozen separately. Yolks should be mixed gently after separating, using sugar or salt as for whole eggs. Egg whites need no special preparation other than the addition of sugar or salt, or if a specially smooth texture is preferred the mixture can be sieved. Whites will whip up successfully after freezing if allowed to reach room temperature first. Hard-boiled eggs should not be frozen as they will go leathery and tough after more than a few days in the freezer.

Butter and cheese can be frozen simply by overwrapping the commercial packages in polythene or moisture-vapour-proof paper and sealing well. Hard cheese may become slightly crumbly in storage after a few weeks. Grated cheese freezes well, and if packed in small usable amounts is ready, after thawing, for adding to sauces, soups and egg dishes.

Cream can be successfully frozen provided it has a butter-fat content of at least 40 per cent and has been pasteurized. Adding sugar will increase the storage life and help to stop separation of liquids and solids. Use 1 tablespoon of sugar to each pint of cream.

*Table 9   Dairy foods*

| | PREPARATION | PACKAGING | HIGH QUALITY STORAGE LIFE MONTHS |
|---|---|---|---|
| *Eggs*<br>Whole | Mix yolks and whites with sugar, ½ tablespoon to 6 eggs or salt, ¼ teaspoon to 6 eggs | Pack in wax cartons or tubs. Seal well. Label with quantity and whether packed in sugar or salt | 9 |
| Yolks | Mix gently, add sugar or salt as for whole egg | As for whole eggs | 9 |
| Whites | Sieve if liked. Add sugar or salt as for whole egg | As for whole eggs | 9 |
| *Butter*<br>Salted and unsalted | Wrap in greaseproof paper if not already wrapped | Wrap in polythene or moisture-vapour-proof paper. Seal well | 3–6 |
| *Cheese*<br>Soft<br>Hard | Wrap in foil or greaseproof paper | As for butter | 4<br>6 |
| *Cream* | Mix with sugar, 1 tablespoon to 1 pint | Pack in wax cartons or tubs. Seal well | 3 |
| *Ice cream* | Home-made should be well beaten while freezing | Store bought ice cream in original packet, if undamaged. Home-made in wax cartons. Seal well | 3 |

# COOKING FOR THE FREEZER

Much of what has already been said about home freezing has applied to the selection and preparation of individual raw foods – vegetables, meat, fish, poultry and game, which will be enjoyed because of their immediate availability in out-of-season months. But frozen foods are very often most appreciated when they require a minimum of time and effort to prepare for the table – and this is achieved by preparing cooked foods for freezing. Frozen dishes need no preparation time before serving other than taking them out of the freezer and re-heating them. They are a boon to the busy businessman when his wife is out for the evening or on holiday, just right for parties or unexpected guests, and a blessing to the housewife at the end of a busy day. From the cook's point of view a lot of time can be spent preparing and cooking one dish – but only a little extra effort is needed to cook two or three times the amount needed for one meal; one for eating and two for the freezer will save time in preparation and cooking at a later date. Time saved in this way is particularly valuable to women who run a home and go out to work. Many housewives have a particular day of the week to bake cakes, scones, pastries and pies – this can be stretched to once a fortnight or more if twice the amount is made and one or two cooked batches put into the freezer.

The quantity of cooked dishes prepared for the freezer will, of course, depend upon the size of the freezer and the number in the family, as well as the individual tastes and requirements. Many families, particularly those with access to freshly picked fruit and vegetables and recently caught fish, may prefer to stock their freezer with these foods, while others will prefer to have a short-term stock of ready meals to help good menu planning when feeding the family.

The wide range of prepared cooked foods which can be frozen at home covers everything from bread, rolls, fruit tarts, scones and cakes to soups, casseroles and roasts, and, for the more adventurous, dishes like goulash, coq au vin, boeuf stroganoff, sole véronique, paellas, and there are many more exciting dishes. The stock for future menus can cover items for breakfast, lunch, tea and dinner.

The advantages of prepared cooked food are exploited by most of the world airlines, ensuring that the air hostesses need only heat up complete meals which were prepared by chefs and frozen some days before. More and more restaurateurs, cafeteria-operators, industrial and hospital caterers have central kitchens, where many of their speciality dishes are prepared in large volume, quick-frozen and distributed to their restaurants and dining rooms–ready for thawing and service as cold sweets and desserts, or for rapid heating or 'end-cooking'.

In view of the wide range of pre-cooked foods now available on the retail market, it might well be assumed that all dishes can be cooked normally, and that if they are frozen and held at a low temperature, they will be completely successful. Some pre-cooked foods, however, are changed by freezing. There are also some foods – plain cooked rice is an example – which do not justify the amount of preparation required. Even though rice freezes very well, the time and fuel used to reheat it is about the same as for cooking freshly when required.

The majority of cooked foods can be frozen without marked changes during freezing and after storage, but there are some which are changed in structure, though relatively simple alternatives in the recipe can make them completely suitable for home freezing. This group includes most sauces, gravies, cream soups, creamed fish and poultry dishes. The reason for this is that freezing causes the water content to crystallize as ice which separates from the oils and fatty solids. On thawing, they cannot always be emulsified again, even by vigorous stirring. Because of the separation of the water as ice, some change in the protein takes place. As most recipes for this group of foods include a thickening agent, separation is less likely to occur if a waxy thickener, preferably cornflour, is used instead of wheat flour. Potatoes and pasta should be omitted when preparing composite dishes. Both of these foods will become soft and mushy and may lose flavour if overcooked, so it is better to add them freshly cooked to meals being re-heated for serving.

There are some other cooked dishes which are excellent immediately after freezing, but have a very short storage life and deteriorate in flavour and texture very quickly, unless held at a very low temperature (certainly lower than that provided by the average home freezer). This group of cooked foods includes dishes containing oily fish such as salmon, most cooked shell fish, offal, bacon, ham, luncheon meat and poultry livers.

Finally there are some foods which deteriorate in texture and flavour so much that it is not worth freezing them. This group includes the following foods:

Custards, including custard tarts and pies.
Cooked egg whites.

Boiled potatoes.
Sour cream.
Mayonnaise.
Stuffed poultry.

*Seasonings* Some seasonings and spices react differently to freezing, and there is no general rule except to use them sparingly during preparation. The flavour of cloves and garlic may become stronger. Pepper and sage seem to increase in flavour during storage; on the other hand salt and onion lose flavour. Curry powder and chilli powder may go musty if dishes containing them are stored too long. It is therefore best to add less seasoning than required and then adjust dishes according to taste when re-heating the food.

## PREPARATION OF COOKED MEATS

In general, prepare the food in the usual way, making such changes to the recipes as is suggested in the more detailed guidance which follows. Just as in the selection of raw foods, all ingredients must be very fresh, and care should be taken that all kitchen utensils used are scrupulously clean. The normal cooking time should be reduced by about one third for foods that will be re-heated before serving; the shorter cooking time not only saves fuel but increases the likely high-quality storage life. After cooking, all food for the freezer should be kept covered and must be cooled rapidly. Dishes of food can be cooled quickly in iced or cold water, but take care that they are cooled sufficiently before plunging them into the cold water, or they may break, unless the dishes are heat and cold resistant. Chilling cooked foods in this way will stop the cooking and help to preserve the natural colour, flavour and texture. Just as soon as the food has cooled it should be packaged, sealed, labelled and frozen.

Home-cooked frozen foods provide a great field for experiments and for many people a home freezer also provides more time to do this and to try out new recipes. Bearing in mind the comments regarding changes in various foods, well tried and favourite recipes, or new ones taken from a magazine or cookery book, can be prepared for the freezer.

The following dishes under group headings will give some idea of the range of cooked foods which are suitable for freezing and contain hints and suggestions for other, similar dishes.

## SOUPS, GRAVIES AND SAUCES

*Suggestions for the freezer*

*Tomato soup. Mixed vegetable soup. Lentil soup. Lobster bisque. Oxtail soup.*

*Consommé. Concentrated meat, chicken or fish stocks. Vichysoisse.*

*Bolognese sauce. Apple sauce. Cranberry sauce. Tomato sauce. Sweet and sour sauce. Cheese sauce. White sauce. Béchamel sauce. Brown gravy. Espagnole sauce. Savoury butters.*

*Preparation* Prepare according to the recipe, but where thickening is required use cornflour for longer-term storage. For cream soups and sauces omit cream and add it when re-heating.

Undercook rather than overcook soups with sliced vegetables, omit potato and pasta, and add these freshly cooked while reheating. Add less seasoning than required and adjust when re-heating.

*Packaging* Leave to cool and remove excess fat from soup and gravy. Pour into wax or foil cartons, using sizes to suit family requirements. Leave $\frac{1}{2}$ in. headspace then cover, seal and label.

*High-quality storage life* Up to 4 months.

*Thawing and serving* Thaw out slightly by dipping package into warm water to release the block. Heat slowly in a saucepan or double boiler. If separation does occur, beat the mixture briskly.

Add cream, potatoes, pasta and seasoning as required.

## STEWS AND CASSEROLES

*Suggestions for the freezer*

*Beef stew. Beef olives. Lamb hot-pot. Chicken casserole. Coq au vin. Goulash. Boeuf stroganoff. Partridge or pheasant casserole. Mince steak in gravy. Curried beef and chicken. Veal fricassée.*

*Preparation* Prepare according to the recipe, but omit potatoes, pasta and bacon. If there are vegetables in the recipe, add these later while cooking, so that they are not overcooked. Add less seasoning than required and adjust while re-heating. Remove from the heat $\frac{1}{3}$ before complete cooking time, as this will be added on when the food is being re-heated for serving.

Cool quickly and keep covered. The dish can be put into cold water after it has slightly cooled to avoid the dish breaking.

*Packaging* Put into meal-size wax or foil cartons or a foil-lined casserole dish. Leave 1 in. headspace. Cover, seal and label.

*High-quality storage life* Up to 3 months.

*Thawing and serving* If the food is in a wax or foil carton, thaw it out slightly, then turn into a saucepan or oven-proof casserole; alternatively, the foil carton can be put straight into the oven. If it is wrapped in foil, remove the foil and put the frozen block into a casserole. Re-heat in the oven or over a low heat.

Add cooked potatoes, pasta or extra seasoning as required.

## MEAT, POULTRY AND GAME

*Suggestions for the freezer*

*Joints of beef, lamb, pork and veal. Chops, cutlets and steaks. Meat loaves and galantines. Whole and/or joints of chicken, duck and turkey. Whole game birds – pheasant, grouse, partridge, etc.*

Although meat, poultry and game to be roasted are better frozen raw and cooked after freezing, a roast joint or bird is a useful stand-by to have in the freezer. Remember that it will take some time to thaw out before it is easy to carve.

Cooked joints or poultry can be sliced, packed in family-size portions, and covered with a sauce or gravy. They have then only to be heated to provide a quick meal.

*Preparation* Cook meat, poultry or game as usual. Roast beef to the rare or medium rare stage if it is to be frozen whole, then, if it is to be re-heated, it won't be overdone. Roast pork should always be well cooked before freezing. Do not stuff poultry or game; the stuffing should be prepared and frozen separately.

Large birds – roast turkey, for example – should be sliced or jointed before packing, otherwise they may not freeze through to the centre. Remove all excess fat from poultry, as it may cause rancidity after a short period of storage.

If packing sliced meats, cover them with a sauce or gravy, otherwise they will dry out quickly and become tough and unpleasant to eat. Cool in a covered container as quickly as possible before freezing.

*Packaging* Wrap whole joints and birds in moisture-vapour-proof paper or a double layer of foil. To prevent bones from puncturing the wrapping, cover with muslin or grease-proof paper beforehand.

Pack sliced meats in flat wax or foil cartons with cooled sauce or gravy poured over. Leave 1 in. headspace, cover, seal and label.

*High-quality storage life* Up to 2 months.

*Thawing and serving* Whole joints and birds: Leave the wrapping on and leave them to thaw in a cool place or in the refrigerator for at least 12–24 hours, depending on the size. If they are to be served hot, remove the original wrapping, cover with foil and roast for $\frac{1}{2}$–1 hour at 350°F (Gas mark 4).

Sliced meats and poultry: Thaw sufficiently to remove from the carton, unless in foil. Put in a casserole and re-heat in the oven. Don't overcook, otherwise the meat may become tough.

Pâtés and meat loaves: Leave for several hours in a cool place until thawed out sufficiently to slice.

## MEAT, FISH AND POULTRY PIES

*Suggestions for the freezer*

*Steak and kidney pies and puddings. Cornish pasties. Minced steak pies. Chicken or game pies. Fish pies. Vol-au-vent or bouchée cases. Pork pies. Pizzas.*

*Preparation* The fillings should be cooked before covering with pastry. For crisper pastry it is better to freeze it uncooked.

Prepare the fillings, see recommendations for stews and casseroles, then leave to cool before covering with pastry.

Pies or tarts can be made in foil pie plates or oven-proof glass dishes or plates.

Vol-au-vent or bouchée cases can be prepared and frozen

uncooked, but it is probably more convenient to freeze them cooked, when they will be ready to re-heat and fill.

*Packaging* Wrap the pies in moisture-vapour-proof paper or foil; seal and label.

*High-quality storage life* Up to 3 months.

*Thawing and serving* There is no need to thaw pies before baking. Remove the wrapping and bake according to the temperature in the recipe.

If using an oven-glass dish, leave it at room temperature for about ½ hour before baking, to avoid a sudden rise in temperature which could cause the glass to crack.

If the pastry starts to brown too quickly, reduce the oven temperature slightly, so that the filling is hot when the pastry is cooked.

FISH

*Suggestions for the freezer*

*Kedgeree. Sole bonne femme. Sole mornay. Poached salmon steaks. Fried fillets, cod, plaice, sole, etc. Trout meunière. Fried scampi.*

*Preparation* Bake, grill, fry or steam fish according to the recipe. If a sauce is required, follow the recommendations in the sauce section. If the fish is coated, egg and breadcrumbs are better: a batter coating may go soft. Use fresh oil or fat for frying, to help prevent off-flavours and rancidity, and drain before packing.

*Packaging* Pack in flat wax or foil cartons. For fried, grilled and baked fish interleave each layer with greaseproof or foil paper. For individual meals wrap cooked fillets separately. If the fish is covered with a sauce, leave $\frac{1}{2}$ in. headspace. Cover the pack, seal and label.

*High-quality storage life* Up to 3 months.

*Thawing and serving* If the fish is in a sauce, thaw out slightly before removing from a wax container; a foil container can be put straight into the oven. Re-heat in a moderate oven, taking care not to overcook the fish.

Grilled or fried fish can be put under a hot grill or in a frying pan for re-heating.

Poached or steamed fish should be left to thaw out if it is to be served cold. If it is required hot, cover it with foil and re-heat it in a steamer or saucepan.

SWEETS AND PUDDINGS

*Suggestions for the freezer*

*Stewed fruit. Fruit purée. Fruit salad. Hot and cold soufflés. Mousse and creams. Trifle. Fruit tarts and pies. Lemon meringue pie. Fruit flans.   Steamed and baked sponge puddings. Milk, rice, semolina, bread and butter puddings.*

*Preparation* Prepare according to the recipe.

For fresh fruit salad, see the section on freezing fruit (page 82). Leave out fruits that are not suitable for freezing, such as bananas, and add them just before serving.

It is better to cook the filling for pies and tarts and cool it before covering it with pastry. If the pie is to be served hot it is better to freeze the pastry uncooked, although a few cooked fruit tarts can be a useful stand-by ready to serve after thawing.

For flans with fruit or other filling, such as lemon, bake the flan case, prepare the filling, and fill the pastry case when cool; then freeze. If a meringue topping is required, freeze the unbeaten egg whites separately. Steamed and baked puddings should be prepared and cooked according to the recipe. Steamed sponge puddings may be frozen uncooked, but there may be a loss of volume and texture after a few months' storage.

Uncooked soufflés can be frozen, provided they are put into the freezer as soon as possible after the whipped egg whites are folded in.

*Packaging* Pack cold sweets in family-size or individual portions in foil or wax cartons.

Pies and tarts can be made in oven-glass dishes or plates. When they are frozen, remove tarts and wrap them in moisture-vapour-proof paper or foil, alternatively make them in foil pie plates or dishes.

Steamed puddings can be left in the basin, or removed when cool and wrapped in foil or moisture-vapour-proof paper. Baked milk puddings should be left in the dish for freezing. They can be removed and wrapped as for tarts.

Soufflés should be kept in the dish after freezing and wrapped in foil or moisture-vapour-proof paper. Seal all wrappings or cartons and label.

*High-quality storage life* 6 months.

*Thawing and serving* Thaw cold sweets in their containers. Allow 1–3 hours at normal room temperature.

Hot puddings may be re-heated straight from the freezer. If the pudding is not in a foil container or oven dish, remove the wrapping and replace the pudding in the dish in which it was originally prepared.

## BREAD, CAKES AND BISCUITS

*Suggestions for the freezer*

*Victoria sandwich. Sponge cake. Plain and rich fruit cakes. Ginger bread. Eclairs. Shortbread. Biscuits. Scones. Bread and rolls. Sandwiches.*

*Preparation* Whereas pastry is better frozen uncooked, cakes and bread retain their texture and flavour more if they are cooked before freezing. With uncooked bread dough the raising properties of the yeast may be less effective and uncooked cake mixtures may lose some volume because the raising agent may not be as effective.

Shortbreads and biscuits may be satisfactorily frozen, cooked or uncooked, but for ease and convenience it is better to freeze them cooked. Prepare them according to the recipe and leave them to cool before wrapping.

Cakes can be filled and iced before freezing or after thawing, but if a frosting or royal icing is required it is better to add this after thawing, as icings go soft and spongy during freezing.

*Packaging* It is easier to wrap soft cakes, such as sponge cake, after the cake is frozen. If freezing layers of a sandwich cake place a piece of moisture-vapour-proof paper between each layer to prevent sticking.

Iced and filled cakes should be frozen before wrapping so that the icing doesn't stick to the paper.

Wrap large cakes in moisture-vapour-proof paper or foil. Small cakes, biscuits and scones can be packed in a wax carton with a piece of moisture-vapour-proof paper between each layer or wrapped as for large cakes.  -

After wrapping, seal and label each carton or packet.

Bread and rolls should be wrapped as above or in polythene bags, and if commercially wrapped they can be put in a polythene bag.

Made sandwiches can be frozen and are particularly useful when preparing for a party. The recommendations given at the beginning of this chapter regarding unsuitable foods for freezing, (p. 105), should be noted when preparing sandwich fillings, unless the sandwiches are for short-term storage.

*High-quality storage life* Up to 6 months.

*Thawing and serving* Rich fruit cakes should be left to thaw out overnight, others take 1–3 hours. Bread can be toasted immediately, and rolls should be taken out 1–2 hours before required.

Some Manufacturers and Main Distributors of Home Freezers

Advance Domestic Appliances
Ltd
18 Berners Street
London W1A 4LH

Bejam Bulk Buying Ltd
Honeypot Lane
Stanmore
Middlesex

Bosch Ltd
Rhodes Way
Radlett Road
Watford WD2 4LB
Hertfordshire

British Domestic Appliances Ltd
(G.E.C., English Electric,
Hotpoint)
Peterborough

Combat Domestic Appliances
(Linde)
New Road
Pershore
Worcestershire

Electrolux Ltd
Luton
Bedfordshire

Electrolux (Commercial
Equipment) Ltd
Porters Wood
Valley Road
St Albans
Hertfordshire

Esta Freeze Ltd
14 Hainton House
Hainton Square
Grimsby

Everest Refrigeration Co. Ltd
506–508 Kingsbury Road
Kingsbury
London N.W.9

Frigidaire Division of General
Motors Ltd
Stag Lane
Kingsbury
London N.W.9

Hoover Ltd
Perivale
Greenford
Middlesex

Prestcold Ltd
Theale
Reading RG7 4AF
Berkshire

Philips Electrical Ltd
Century House
Shaftesbury Avenue
London W.C.2

Thorn Domestic Appliances
(Electrical) Ltd
New Lane
Havant P09 2NH
Hampshire

Total Refrigeration Ltd
46 Gorst Road
London N.W.10

The manufacturers and importers given above will supply literature and information on home freezers for domestic and/or commercial use. Literature and brochures may also be obtained from many electrical appliance retailers, departmental stores and electricity service centres.

# MORE ABOUT PENGUINS

*Penguinews*, which appears every month, contains
details of all the new books issued by Penguins as they
are published. From time to time it is supplemented by
*Penguins in Print* – a complete list of all our available
titles. (There are well over three thousand of these.)

A specimen copy of *Penguinews* will be sent to you
free on request, and you can become a subscriber for the
price of the postage – 30p for a year's issues (including the
complete lists) if you live in the United Kingdom, or
60p if you live elsewhere. Just write to Dept EP,
Penguin Books Ltd, Harmondsworth, Middlesex,
enclosing a cheque or postal order, and your name will
be added to the mailing list.
Some other Penguin Handbooks are described on the
following pages.

Note: *Penguinews* and *Penguins in Print* are **not**
available in the U.S.A. or Canada

# THE PENGUIN COOKERY BOOK

*Bee Nilson*

'My choice for a young housewife's first cook book –
particularly if she is tied to a strict budget – is *The
Penguin Cookery Book* by Bee Nilson' – Ambrose Heath
in *Ideal Home*.

'A book which is likely to find a grateful and useful
place in many homes ... Here are some 850 basic
recipes, given in both weights and measures, indexed
and cross-referenced ... Should the beginner require
more than that, he or she will also find advice on kitchen
equipment, food values, how much food to buy for how
many, cooking time, temperatures, and a glossary of
French terms. Finally there are diagrams, to assist in
identifying the different cuts of meat and in preparing
fish' – *Listener*

# LEAVE IT TO COOK
# THE SLOW COOKING METHOD

*Stella Atterbury*

The Slow Cooking Method, in which dishes are cooked
for as much as eight hours or longer, can be used on
most cookers and has obvious advantages: meals can be
left to cook without attention for the whole day or
night; food will retain its natural flavours and juices
through being cooked at low temperature by filling the
oven to capacity dishes for several days can be cooked at
one session, thus saving time and expense.

In this new Penguin Handbook Stella Atterbury
includes special recipes for soups, fish, meats, casseroled
dishes, vegetables, savouries, sweets, preserves and
oven stop-gaps – all of which take the minimum
amount of time to prepare. In the last section she
describes recipes for sauces and stuffings which can be
made quickly to complement the slowly cooked dish.
Helpful to all cooks, this book is especially valuable for
those who must be away from home all day.

# SOUPS AND HORS D'OEUVRES

*Marika Hanbury Tenison*

'No experiments with the first course,' most cooks
say, 'better to be safe than sorry.'

They don't know what they're missing, and this book
tells you why. With a little help from Marika Hanbury
Tenison you can add a dash of imagination to the
simplest soup or salad dish, and on the important
occasion you can be really flamboyant. All the classic
dishes are here, but when you tire of smoked salmon,
trout, avocado, prawn cocktail, pâté or moules
marinières you can always try something completely
new – one of the many recipes in the book which have
until now been well-kept secrets in Mrs Hanbury
Tenison's kitchen. As well as dishes from all over the
world there is helpful advice about linking the first
course with the rest of the meal; and there are also
original suggestions for preparing enticing party eats'

# GOOD FOOD ON A BUDGET

*Georgina Horley*

Rousseau's reputed recipe for happiness was: a good
bank account, a good cook, and a good digestion.
Mindful of the shortcomings of modern government
*Good Food on a Budget* dispenses with the first
ingredient.

Georgina Horley belongs to the depressed majority who
manage on modest budgets and, apart from being a
writer, is a Cordon Bleu instructor in cookery. She has
assembled in this Penguin a mass of advice, tabulated
information, and recipes which can help wives, mothers,
and others who have interests beyond the cooker and the
kitchen sink and for whom time and money are the
enemies. Against the former she draws up an array of
convenience foods, kitchen-gadgets (where justified),
cake-making ready-reckoners, tables, and 'good-quick-
'n'-easy' recipes. Against the latter her principal weapon
is a study of the seasons, with food calendars which
indicate the best buys in the local shops at each time of
year.
With few exceptions these recipes have been made
repeatedly by the author and fed to *gourmets*: and they
have come again. So to hell with wealth! And if you can't
be a good cook, then marry one.